The
Radical
Imperative

FROM THEOLOGY TO SOCIAL ETHICS

by
John C. Bennett

THE WESTMINSTER PRESS
Philadelphia

Scripture quotations from the Revised Standard Version of the Bible are copyright, 1946 and 1952, by the Division of Christian Education of the National Council of Churches, and are used by permission.

Book Design by Dorothy Alden Smith

Published by The Westminster Press ®
Philadelphia, Pennsylvania

PRINTED IN THE UNITED STATES OF AMERICA

3 4 5 6 7 8 9

To our grandchildren

Elizabeth Ann
Catherine Anne
Anita Louise
John Christopher

Library of Congress Cataloging in Publication

Bennett, John Coleman, 1902–
    The radical imperative.

    Includes bibliographical references.
    1. Christian ethics. 2. Social ethics. I. Title.
BJ1251.B43   241   75–15538
ISBN 0–664–20824–X
ISBN 0–664–24769–5 pbk.

Contents

Preface

The use of the word "radical" in the title may be best explained by referring to perceptions and convictions that have led me to write this book. I believe there is need to reaffirm the Christian radical social imperative in the light of the present plight of humanity, and of the divisive controversies in many churches concerning their social responsibility. What I have written represents a new stage in my lifelong argument with forms of Christianity that have encouraged religious privatism or given Christian sanction to the ways of the dominant institutions and powers in the Western world.

I am shaken as never before by the realization that the majority of people in the world live in conditions of severe deprivation and are victims of poverty and very often of famine. Gustavo Gutiérrez in *A Theology of Liberation* has described the situation well when he says, "It is only in the last few years that people have become clearly aware of the scope of misery and especially of the oppressive and alienating circumstances in which the great majority of mankind exists" (p. 64). If we take seriously the claims of social justice on a global scale, we are bound to engage in the profoundest criticisms of the presuppositions of the way of life in our country and in most countries of the northern hemisphere.

I see the need to transform the use of American power in the world. This would involve abandonment of the role of the

United States as guardian of the *status quo* for the sake of our economic interests, of being the habitual opponent of revolutions abroad, of being the great power that is the special friend of cruel rightist tyrannies in the interest either of "anti-Communism" or of maintaining stability as the value of highest priority. The consensus that controlled foreign policy for more than two decades was a product of the early cold war. This consensus—which expressed the assumption that American predominance in the world belonged to the nature of things—has lost credibility; but it still has influence on national attitudes and policy. Changes will come as events push us to respond in new ways to the limits of our power and resources. It will be good for all if the American people accept the loss of predominance with understanding and without being too much tempted by isolationism.

I see the failure of American economic institutions at home to achieve greater equality or to overcome the shameful poverty of twenty-five to thirty million of our own people. The next stage in the struggle for justice should emphasize the special economic handicaps of racial minorities and women. A more fundamental critique of the presuppositions of American economic institutions is called for than that connected with the many good reforms of recent decades.

It is out of these perceptions and convictions that "radical" gets its meaning. How they are related to what I regard as essential Christian teaching is suggested in the first two chapters.

What about the meaning of "imperative"? I do not see this as an external, or arbitrary, imposition on humanity of an alien demand by God. The question is often raised when moral imperatives are discussed: Does God will something because it is good, or is it good because God wills it? I do not believe that God's will is alien to the nature of creation. I see this question as posing a false dilemma. We discover the will of God in part from a better understanding of the needs of God's people. Insofar as the Christian revelation provides a clue to God's will and to the nature of creation it is unique and irreplaceable; but it is not isolated. Fortunately there is support for many Christian moral insights from those who live by other commitments. The Biblical revelation with Christ as the center, to which I often appeal in this book, may still be tested by the extent to which it illumines the mysteries of our existence, the conflicts of value, the abysses of evil, and conscientious perceptions of goodness, justice, and social health. On these Christians have no monopoly.

We cannot live by imperatives alone. By themselves they often drive us to despair. The God of the radical imperative, however, is also the God of grace and forgiveness. Implications of the radical imperative are seen in the comprehensiveness of God's love, which is prior to judgment upon sins against love. The God of the radical imperative is also the God whose redemptive acts are described in the indicative mood. I give some attention to this dimension in Chapter IV, but I realize that it needs vastly more emphasis so long as it does not undercut the essential force of the radical imperative.

There is a strong temptation to respond to the radical imperative by retreating into the idea of complexity made the more intimidating by awareness of the depth of history's tragedy and the pervasiveness of sin. I know that particular changes in laws, institutions, and policies cannot be deduced from any imperative alone. Many sources of knowledge and insight, and even of motive, are needed. Living with a sense of wrongs to be righted and with full realization of the complexity involved in finding ways to right them is our fate and our responsibility. The form the imperative takes in each situation should both prod consciences to find the way to new policies and programs, and project the vision that draws and inspires.

I recognize in myself a too bland acceptance of national trends in the 1940's and 1950's. The fact that there was considerable harmony between my ethical convictions and the policies of the United States Government during the Second World War and during the early years of the cold war contributed to this, as did my tendency to be overly optimistic about the effects of the "mixed economy." In some respects I believe that the spirit of this book is closer to that of my first book, *Social Salvation*, published almost exactly forty years ago, than it is to many things I have written during the intervening years. I hope this work benefits from much that I have learned during those years!

I am a product of both the social gospel and of Christian realism. I owe a great debt to the ecumenical bodies with which I have worked for decades, and this debt is reflected in Chapter III. I also owe a great debt to my thirty-one years at Union Theological Seminary as student, teacher, and administrator, particularly to many colleagues and students. The ethos of the Union community has preserved a remarkable continuity amid great changes. My experience of nearly five years at Pacific School of Religion and the Graduate Theological Union since 1970 has been rich with similar experiences, especially the stimulus and inspiration that come from ecumenical diversity.

These chapters are not published lectures or republished articles, although many such previous efforts belong to their history. Chapter IV carries to a new stage the thought in my article, given the exaggerated title "Two Christianities," in *Worldview*, October 1973. Of the many occasions on which I have given lectures that contributed to these chapters I mention with gratitude visits to the Faculty of Religious Studies, McGill University, where I gave the Birks Lectures, to St. Andrew's College in Saskatoon, to the Southeastern Baptist Theological Seminary, where I gave the Carver-Barnes Lectures, and to the United Theological Seminary of the Twin Cities, in New Brighton, Minnesota.

J. C. B.

Claremont, California

I
Sources
of the Radical Imperative

There is a Christian imperative to seek justice and peace. It is a mandate that requires a radical dealing with the problems of public life, the structures and institutions of society, the policies of governments, and political movements for change. This radical imperative is a reflection of the love of God for all people, and human response to it is an expression of love for all neighbors. It does not prescribe particular ideologies, systems, institutions, and policies, but it puts a heavy burden of proof on all of these as they determine our choices. When I say "our," the word is left somewhat open. Those who share Christian presuppositions can claim no monopoly on the moral insights, sensitivities, and commitments that enter into the response to this imperative. However much others may differ in their understanding of its ground, the imperative is not an alien, arbitrary command, but there are many pointers to it in our common experience, and it often corresponds to the leadings of conscience.

FIVE SOURCES OF THE RADICAL IMPERATIVE

I shall now describe five sources of our understanding of the radical imperative, and this will tell a great deal about its content. These five sources involve indicatives, and I want to make it clear from the beginning that the imperative is implied in indicatives that are affirmations about God and about humanity.

1. The first is faith in God's involvement with humanity in history. We see his identification with the whole human race in Christ. This was preceded by his covenant with Israel dramatized in the exodus, which is a paradigm for the liberation of oppressed people. It is given expression by the prophets in their emphasis upon social justice. I believe that we can start with the assumption that God is concerned about the public life of humanity and not only about the inner, private life of individuals, that he is concerned about nations and events and not only about the salvation of souls.

We may best realize the importance of this assumption if we compare it with conceptions of God that stress his self-sufficient detachment from time and change and history. There has always been serious tension between classical ideas of divine perfection in which God is unaffected by the strivings and sufferings of his creatures, and God as he is revealed in the Bible as struggling with the rebellions of his people and as suffering as the result of their disobedience. This suffering of the involved God is portrayed in the cross of Christ. Today I seldom hear of attempts to separate the human nature of Christ, which suffers, from the divine nature of Christ, which has at times been believed to be free from suffering. That kind of theological manipulation of the two natures of Christ has lost what power to convince it may have had at other times when the concern to preserve the detached bliss of the divine perfection was paramount in theory. Changes in theology are often deeper than those which are debated most explicitly. One of the changes that I find on all sides is the abandonment of belief in the divine impassibility, or the freedom of God from being affected by what happens in his changing creation, especially by the suffering of his creatures.

2. The second source of the radical social imperative is the assumption that human beings are both material and

spiritual. They are not to be understood as souls that can be separated either from bodies or from communities. The Christian concern about salvation now is concern for whole persons in communities. One of the great Christian leaders of the first half of this century was William Temple, Archbishop of Canterbury, a forceful advocate of Christian responsibility for economic justice. He used to say that "Christianity is the most avowedly materialist of all the world's religions."[1] He said this because of the fact of the incarnation, because of the religious and ethical importance of action in the material world, because of the "ultimate significance of the historical process." It has often been emphasized that there is significance in the inclusion of the petition for daily bread in the Lord's Prayer.

All of this has fortunately become platitudinous. I believe that we can see its importance in fresh ways today because we better understand how vulnerable persons are to the influences of the material environment, especially in the earliest and most determinative years. I remember the shock that I felt when I first learned that malnutrition during the first six months of a child's life may damage the mental development of the child irreversibly. Could there be a clearer sign of the unity of the person, body and soul, in the community? When we see this grim threat to children in the light of what we know about the prevalence of malnutrition and hunger in the world today we see with great vividness how this understanding of the nature of persons controls our responsibility for radical social change. This responsibility is basically political, based upon well-known facts seen in the light of a theological view of persons.

3. The third source, which I might have developed in my discussion of God's involvement, is belief in God's aggressive love for all persons. I discuss this separately, though it is implied in my first point, because there is an extraordinarily broad agreement among theologians today on one extension of this belief. It is the conviction that God's love for all per-

sons implies a strategic concentration on the victims of society, on the weak, the exploited, the neglected persons who
are a large majority of the human race. I use the word
"strategic" because I do not believe that God loves the victims more than he does the beneficiaries of our institutions
and styles of life, but there is need for strategic concentration
on the victims which is analogous to the strategic concentration on the lost sheep in the Gospel parable. I hesitate to use
that analogy, because it might suggest to the careless reader
that somehow, in the spiritual dimension, the victims are
more lost than those who are comfortable! The announce-
ment that God concentrates on society's victims may strike
the comfortable as suggesting that God is indeed partial.

It seems clear to me that an emphasis on divine partiality
understood in this strategic sense is an implication of the
much-loved story of the last judgment in Matt., ch. 25. The
identification of Christ with the hungry, the thirsty, the
stranger (or refugee), the naked, the sick, and the imprisoned
loses its implications for political and social policy when we
think of marginal individuals who need help one by one. But
the story becomes radically political when we realize that it
refers to more than a billion persons in the world at large and
to more than thirty million persons in affluent America.

One of the reasons for this widespread agreement on the
partiality of God toward the victims of society is that most
large groups of victims are now being heard from. Their
spokesmen speak within the churches as well as to the
churches on a scale that is new. They have often gained
enough power to push. In the case of the industrial workers
in Western countries we see how one group has gained
power to change social structures to some extent in its favor.
Black people in the United States have very articulate
spokesmen who have put white Americans on the moral
defensive, and black theology has helped white theologians
to become aware of their cultural and racial blind spots.
Women who have been denied equal opportunity with men

in society and who have been victims of the patriarchal tradition of the churches have in recent years caused men to think new thoughts. Already changes have come in the laws of the state, in the practices of educational institutions and corporations, and in thinking about theological and liturgical symbols in churches. The struggles for justice in the Third World have had a profound effect on the ecumenical outlook in the churches. The World Council of Churches has become a sounding board for the aspirations of the Third World, and strong currents in the Roman Catholic Church move in the same direction. This list of trends may suggest to some readers that I believe theology should move with any popular tide. Not at all. What I am asking is that theology listen to new voices to correct its identification for many centuries with those who represent the powers in the world of privileged white men in Europe and North America.

On this issue I call as a witness one who was not identified with the American social gospel traditions and who was himself deeply concerned to keep theology from being the servant of any culture—Karl Barth. I have never been in his theological camp, but I have appreciated the way in which, before most theologians, he came to emphasize the form of divine partiality of which I have been speaking. He first gave me the courage to speak of it. I shall quote two passages from Barth. He says: "God always takes his stand unconditionally and passionately on this side and on this side alone: against the lofty and on behalf of the lowly; against those who already enjoy right and privilege and on behalf of those who are denied it and deprived of it."[2] The other passage, from an essay written in 1946, gave me the idea of the analogy between God's strategic concentration on the victims of society and the Gospel parable concerning the lost sheep. Barth writes: "The Church is witness of the fact that the Son of God came to seek and to save the lost. And this implies that —casting all false impartiality aside—the Church must concentrate first on the lower and lowest levels of human society. The poor, the socially and economically weak and threatened, will always be the object of its primary and particular concern, and it will always insist on the state's special responsibility for these weaker members of society."[3] That last sentence indicates that Barth does not see the church's responsibility in terms of traditional forms of charity but as also requiring political action.

Pope Paul VI, in his encyclical *Populorum Progressio,* in many ways expresses this same concern. He quotes the familiar words of St. Ambrose, who said to the rich: "You are not making a gift of your possessions to the poor person. You are handing over to him what is his. For what has been given in common for the use of all, you have arrogated to yourself. The world is given to all and not only to the rich." Then the pope says: "That is, private property does not constitute for anyone an absolute and unconditional right. No one is justified in keeping for his exclusive use what he does not need, when others lack necessities" (par. 23). Admittedly that is a watering down of what Ambrose said, but it goes far beyond what those of us who are among the comfortable in the churches have taken for granted about the rights of property.

4. Next I emphasize the social consequences of sin. Here I refer both to the social consequences of the sins of individuals and the sins that are embodied in social groups and institutions, in the political and cultural principalities and powers that determine so largely the fate of peoples and nations. There are many problems in working out the relationship between guilt, which is the personal responsibility of individuals, and the evil consequences of the behavior of groups and institutions, and of cultural habits, which do much to determine that behavior. For our purpose these issues can remain open so long as both personal responsibility and corporate responsibility are seen to be real and fateful.

One special problem in the relation of personal responsibility to the sins of nations is illustrated very well by the Stuttgart Declaration, in which some leaders of the German churches in 1945 confessed their guilt for the crimes of their government. In such cases it is usually those who are least responsible personally for the national crimes who have the moral sensitivity and the courage to offer the confession. Those who spoke through the Stuttgart Declaration had struggled at great cost to themselves against the policies of their government. The signers included Martin Niemöller, Bishop Otto Dibelius, Johannes Lilje (later Bishop), and Bishop Theophil Wurm. Two laymen signed it also. One of them, Dr. Gustav Heinemann, later became president of the Federal Republic of Germany. That his election could have come about after his signing that statement speaks well for his fellow citizens. If confessions of the social consequences of sin that now often form a part of the liturgy in churches are to be taken seriously at all, they imply commitment to radical social changes.

The Stuttgart Declaration included the following paragraph:

> We know ourselves to be one with our people in a great company of suffering and in a great solidarity of guilt. With great pain do we say: through us endless suffering has been brought to many peoples and countries. What we have often borne witness to before our congregations, that we now declare in the name of the whole church. True, we have struggled for many years in the name of Jesus Christ against a spirit which found its terrible expression in the National Socialist regime of violence, but we accuse ourselves for not witnessing more courageously, for not praying more faithfully, for not believing more joyously and for not loving more ardently.

Teaching within churches should illumine the self-deceptions that so easily hide our involvement in corporate sin. Also, there is a strategic importance in beginning with the sins of our own group or of our own side in a conflict. Confession can hardly begin with the confession of the sins of others.

The possibility of even seeing the sins on our own side is a great contribution toward preserving openness to persons on the other side. It helps avoid that blinding self-righteousness which exacerbates conflicts and makes ultimate reconciliation between people who are divided impossible.

Dorothee Soelle, in her *Political Theology*, has a chapter on "Sin, Politically Interpreted,"[4] in which she says that sin in a political context is "collaboration and apathy," for the "sinner is the collaborator (seemingly harmless, from the point of view of the natural consciousness) of a structurally founded, usually anonymous injustice." She sees this political understanding of sin as standing in sharp contrast to dominant tendencies in the various theological traditions, for which "the collectives in which we live—nations, races, classes, communities, groups—do not enter the picture." This is one point at which her attack on the *privatism* of conventional Christianity is very strong.

Two thinkers who have done much to form my own mind have greatly stressed both the social consequences of the sins of individuals and the sin embodied in nations, races, and systems. Walter Rauschenbusch and Reinhold Niebuhr cover a great deal of ground in American theology. Rauschenbusch was the greatest representative of the liberal social gospel, and Niebuhr, though in many ways a product of the social gospel, was the most influential critic of its theology. Probably Rauschenbusch's most original contributions to theology were his conception of the transmission of sin through cultural habits and social institutions and his conception of what he called "super-personal forces of evil," unified in "the Kingdom of Evil." He says: "The life of humanity is infinitely interwoven, always renewing itself, yet always perpetuating what has been. The evils of one generation are caused by the wrongs of the generations that preceded, and will in turn condition the sufferings and temptations of those who come after."[5] His writing is full of concrete illustrations of these collective wrongs. He welcomes the solidaristic aspect of the

doctrine of original sin, but he points out that in its stress on
the catastrophe of the fall of Adam "theology has had little
to say about the contributions which our more recent forefa-
thers have made to the sin and misery of mankind."[6]

Reinhold Niebuhr differed from Rauschenbusch in that he
regarded the sin of pride as more fundamental and destructive than the sin of selfishness, but he continually talked
about the pride of nations, races, and classes. He saw how
closely interwoven are self-deception and the deception of
others in the sins of collectives and institutions of all kinds.
One of his most powerful sermons was about the story of the
true prophet, Micaiah, in his relation to Ahab's four hundred
false prophets. He makes the interesting point that Jehosha-
phat, the king of Judah, who at that time was an ally of Ahab,
was able to be suspicious of Ahab's four hundred because
they were Ahab's prophets and not his. Then he adds:

> Each nation sees the hypocrisies of its neighbors with
> cynical penetration: but it usually makes hypocritical
> pretensions of its own in the same breath. The reason
> each nation is so certain that it possesses a higher degree
> of honesty than its neighbors is that what appears as
> hypocrisy from outside is usually only self-deception
> from inside.[7]

Niebuhr's writings deal continually with the theme of collective sin. His *Moral Man and Immoral Society* may well be the
most powerful statement of this subject in the history of
theology. His chapter in that book entitled "The Morality of
Nations" is, unfortunately, timeless. He has much to say
about differences between nations, all of which are sinful in
the sight of God. The demonic malevolence of Nazi Germany
was quite different in his mind from the pride and egoism of
the United States and other nations that were free from such
obsessions. At their best, through minorities within them,
they were open to and influenced by judgments from beyond
themselves. The collective as sinner in concrete, historical

terms has been taken for granted in wide theological and ecclesiastical circles. There have been no better guides to this subject than Walter Rauschenbusch and Reinhold Niebuhr.

The possibility of national confessions of sin leading to reconciliation in situations quite far removed from circles influenced by Christian faith was illustrated recently. The prime minister of Pakistan, Zulfikar Ali Bhutto, during a visit to Bangladesh on June 29, 1974, spoke of the "shameful repression and unbearable horrors" to which the people of Bangladesh had been subjected by the government of his own country. He said: "God has punished us for the sins and transgressions of 1971. The country was sundered and a yawning gap was opened between you and us." It is moving to encounter evidences of grace penetrating the places that have been centers of the most cruel conflict. The fact that such signs of repentance are good statesmanship indicates something of the essential solidarity of humanity that underlies all violations of it.

Theological teaching about the depth and pervasiveness of sin in human life should not be used to discredit any human group or community, though this has often happened. To protect against such a misuse of this teaching in the Christian context one should begin with one's own sin and the sins of one's own group, not with the sins of neighbors or of those in some other camp. "Why do you see the speck that is in your brother's eye, but do not notice the log that is in your own eye?" (Matt. 7:3.) Confession marks the beginning of both charity and wisdom as we approach the problems of social ethics. In keeping before us the dignity and the possibilities of all persons, Christian faith has no illusions about their virtue, for it reminds us of the distortions that come from pride, self-centeredness, and apathy. Yet to begin with the confession of one's own sin may keep the negative teachings about human nature from obscuring the positive teachings. To include ourselves when we generalize about others is likely to limit the negativism. If in principle we were to despair of most people, especially of those who are different from ourselves, the world would indeed be so hopeless a place that we might well conclude that any change would be for the worse.

5. The worldwide inclusiveness of the church provides strong support to all that I have said about the radical social imperative. The church today includes people in almost all nations, and it cuts across the social divisions of race and class. It is present on opposite sides of most ideological conflicts, even though there are conflicts between its faith and some ideological claims. Even when that is so, as in the case of absolutistic Marxism-Leninism, Christians will often identify with the goals of various movements expressing that ideology in contrast to capitalism or the imperialistic impact of Western nations. It is unfortunate that the churches can have only minor influence on the conflict between East and West because in Communist nations their freedom to speak or act in relation to public policy is so completely curtailed. However, in the conflict which is now much deeper and is certain to be persistent between northern and southern hemispheres, between rich and poor nations, the churches do have very important roles on both sides. I shall have more to say in other chapters about the churches in this context as sources of ethical guidance for each other. Here I am concerned to emphasize the reality of the inclusive church as a support for the radical social imperative.

In Paul's beautiful passage about the organic nature of the church as a body he says: "If one member suffers, all suffer together; if one member is honored, all rejoice together" (I Cor. 12:26). Those words express the implications of the Christian love that should be embodied in the worldwide, inclusive church. Since a large proportion of the people in the church are suffering victims of social and political institutions, to be in the church anywhere is to live with that suffering everywhere. Therefore those church members who belong to the privileged and more powerful groups are under strong pressure to learn about the religious and moral implications of that suffering for them. The former understanding of world outreach of the churches in Europe and North America in mission has changed. Those churches now participate in a worldwide ecumenical community that involves listening as well as speaking. Indeed, at this stage, it involves more listening than speaking.

There is also an important addition to this idea of the responsibilities of mutual love within the church. Today, more than has been the case in previous periods, Christians in other nations or on the other side of any dividing line represent not only themselves; they also represent their non-Christian neighbors and the sufferings, needs, aspirations, and destinies of the corporate groups to which they belong. So, to speak of the role of the church in this context initiates us in a remarkable way into the realities of oppression and poverty and hunger that call for radical political change for whole nations and continents.

I shall give two examples of what I mean. The first is a message by Helder Câmara, the Roman Catholic Archbishop of Olinda and Recife in Brazil, addressed to Christians in the northern hemisphere. Câmara is one of the most courageous Christian voices in the world today. It is significant for Americans that he risks his freedom and even his life by his constant struggle against the oppressive government of Brazil, which is one of our Government's favorite regimes in Latin America. In an address to a World Council of Churches consultation on "development" in Montreux, Switzerland, in 1970, Archbishop Câmara said:

> Our responsibility as Christians makes us tremble. The northern hemisphere, the developed area of the world, the 20% who possess 80% of the world's resources, are of Christian origin. What impression can our African and Asian brethren and the masses in Latin America have of

Christianity, if the tree is to be judged by its fruits? For we Christians are largely responsible for the unjust world in which we live. . . .

What a splendid testimony we could give if we were to unite with our Christian brethren in the developed countries to do everything in our power to overcome the egoism of the northern hemisphere—which is the Christian hemisphere, or at any rate Christian in origin![8]

Perhaps today the archbishop would not use the words "developed" and "underdeveloped," which are now being criticized in his circles. Nevertheless, he is expressing the radical demand implicit in the suffering and oppression of the people among whom he lives, a demand upon Christians elsewhere who are more fortunate; and he speaks not only for his fellow Christians in his part of the world but for his people and neighboring peoples without regard to their religious commitments.

My second illustration is from the report of the conference on "Salvation Today" held in Bangkok under the auspices of the World Council of Churches in December 1972. With its 326 representatives from 69 countries, this conference represented among other things the present results of generations of the missionary work of Western churches. Probably this meeting went beyond any previous events in facing the divisions between the churches of countries that over the years have sent missionaries and the churches of countries that over the years have received missionaries. I shall quote two passages from the report of this remarkably inclusive body.

The first deals with the foundation of the struggle for social justice in the gospel:

God's justice manifests itself both in the justification of the sinner and in social and political justice. As guilt is both individual and corporate, so God's liberating power changes both persons and structures. We see the struggles for economic justice, political freedom, and cultural renewal as elements of the total liberation of the world through the mission of God.

This meeting was held under the shadow of the American bombing of the cities of North Vietnam in December 1972, and one passage in the report was clearly addressed to the American churches:

How can we preach the good news of Salvation Today when on the same day a holocaust of destruction is unleashed which is widely believed by its perpetrators to be a defense of freedom and Christian values? How can we discuss a missionary strategy of the Christian Church in our time when millions of Asians are faced with the brutal power politics of countries some of which are made up predominantly of people who profess Christianity?

I think that we can say that only a minority of Christians in the United States in December 1972 believed that the bombing was in any sense a defense of "Christian values." This statement is an excellent example of the kind of radical challenge that members of the worldwide Christian community can express to each other. In this case the challenge was obviously brought not for the sake of Christians but for the sake of the millions of Asians who were victims of that "holocaust of destruction."

I have briefly outlined the implications of five aspects of essential Christian faith that are prior to systematic theological formulations and that are expressed through a variety of such formulations. It seems to me that any one of the five can be a way of seeing the claims of the radical social imperative. And when all five are taken seriously and combined we have an approach to a radical social ethic that cannot be denied or set aside without renouncing aspects of the faith that are essential and compelling. Later, in Chapter IV, I shall deal with the question: Why have the implications of these aspects of our faith been so generally neglected in Christian history?

The Radical Imperative
and Theological Traditions

Major theological traditions are influential in churches that belong to the broad ecumenical community. I think that we can say, however, that these various traditions do not of themselves determine how the radical imperative is to be understood today, or how we should relate that imperative to the problems of social ethics. The edges of the traditions that historically caused deep differences in social attitudes have been largely eroded. One word of caution, suggested by Walter Rauschenbusch, applies to our time with a fresh relevance. In 1907 he wrote: "Eminent theologians, like other eminent thinkers, live in the social environment of wealth and to that extent are slow to see."[9] James Cone and other black theologians would give this a racial twist and say that white theologians are slow to see. And we are continually reminded of the blind spots that have distorted theological perspectives because almost all theologians have been males.

Among the major theological traditions, Calvinism, broadly speaking, has been more favorable to radical social change than has Lutheranism. Yet there has been a great difference between Lutheranism in Scandinavia and Lutheranism in Germany. And in Germany it has changed markedly as authoritarian nationalistic, and indeed militaristic, tendencies have been in large measure overcome. In the United States there are many different positions held among Lutherans, but increasingly I am impressed by the progressive political actions of theologians and leaders of various Lutheran denominations. Calvinism, when allied with an oppressive establishment as in South Africa, can give rise to a pathological conservatism; at the same time there are individuals representing that tradition who have bravely struggled against official doctrines and practices. It would be easy for disciples of Karl Barth to work with Roman Catholics for revolutionary change in Latin America, with the latter getting considerable support from Pope Paul VI's encyclical *Populorum Progressio*. Quakers and Roman Catholics sometimes hold the same positions about war and peace, with Catholics often taking the more radical initiatives. There is great fluidity in theological traditions. Two reasons for this are the pressure of the same events on them all, and the continuous conversation between their representatives as part of the sharing of common Christian commitments that unite them.

I shall give illustrations from the lives of two theologians. Dietrich Bonhoeffer had a very high doctrine of the church. Yet he found that on a deep level of social commitment he had far more in common with Christians of other traditions and even with atheists who opposed National Socialism than he had with fellow Lutherans who used the same words and concepts in theology but who, from his point of view, were collaborators with the Nazi regime. Reinhold Niebuhr used to say to entering students at Union Theological Seminary that he generally found himself working politically with Catholics and Jews against Protestants, though he was a strong exponent of his own form of Reformation theology. As he saw it, Protestants were generally so bogged down in an individualistic "Protestant ethic" that they had little sense of the claims for social justice, while Catholics and Jews were the industrial workers and felt the pinch of oppression. Even affluent Jews had the experience of being a minority that was generally outside the circle of American establishments.

To speak of the weakening of the differences between the major traditions that have been important historically in regard to social ethics does not mean that theological ideas are not socially determinative. Basic Biblical insights that have theological implications lie behind our social commitments. Also, theological ideas that are characteristic of particular schools of thought within churches may inhibit or encourage active expressions of those commitments and may determine both priorities and directions.

There are otherworldly theological outlooks that cause Christians to discount the importance of doing anything about the evils of this world. This is true of vivid expectations of the early second coming of Christ, who will set things right. There are also forms of spiritual individualism that put so much emphasis on the inner life, or on the religious conversion of individuals, or on changes in private life that they lead Christians to discount the importance of corporate or political action. They often assume that converted individuals will be released from the blind spots of their class or race or culture without any special instruction about the nature of those blind spots. The latter assumption has been refuted quite generally by our experience. There are conservative interpretations of divine providence that put such a burden of proof on all radical changes that they are in effect theologically rejected. This is especially true of the very widespread traditional assumption based upon Rom., ch. 13, and other proof texts to the effect that Christians should always obey political authorities. There are forms of theological pessimism among orthodox Protestants that cause them to believe that any change is likely to be for the worse. This is all the more convincing if they happen to enjoy many advantages from the *status quo*. There are also forms of liberal idealism or rationalism or utopianism that have not prepared Christians to deal with the ambiguities involved in most ethical judgments about social or political policy.

One could speak at length about the changes that have come in Roman Catholicism, which are partly theological changes. These deal with the exclusiveness of the church as the custodian of the means of grace, the relation of sin to sins, the place of love in moral theology, specific deductions from natural law, the nature of the authority of the pope, the proper relations between church and state. All the changes make a vast difference in Catholic social ethics and in the impact of Catholicism upon the world. This is an exciting chapter in the history of the church and of Christian theology. *Theology does make an enormous difference to social ethics, but this difference cannot be understood by studying traditional charts on which the lines that relate theology and social ethics are drawn.*

In the next two chapters I shall discuss sources of guidance for Christian social ethics. Emphasis will be on the Bible as the primary record of the revelation of God with Christ as the center, and on important discoveries and processes of corporate thinking in the life of the church.

II
Biblical Sources
of Ethical Guidance

We do not create our own Christian ethics for the 1970's. Yet when it comes to decisions about the issues that we face today we have to make up our own minds. Our situation has elements that are new, even unique, that could not have been imagined by the Biblical writers or by our most influential predecessors in the church. Moreover, we get essential guidance for concrete decisions from many different sources. Much of it comes from contemporary experience, from those sciences which deal both with human affairs and with nature, and from ethical analyses that are independent of Christian ethics (though those who engage in them, even when they have no theological commitments, are often influenced by Christian ethics).

Christian ethics has its own distinctive sources. Its contemporary representatives respond to many new issues and learn from secular sources of information and ethical wisdom, consciously or unconsciously. As they select issues for emphasis they give more weight to some secular sources of guidance than to others. Their minds are formed by a prior commitment and by a prior response to the revelation of God and humanity in the Bible with Christ as its center. This prior response is not a shortcut to solutions of ethical problems today. Indeed it raises many problems of interpretation of its own. Many issues are hidden in the words "with Christ as its center," since the meaning of Christ differs profoundly among Christians. For different groups of Christians he may be the mediator of a private or otherworldly form of salvation; or a lawgiver on such matters as property, violence, and marriage; or a teacher and redeemer of human beings in a sinful world to which absolute moral laws do not apply. He may be a political revolutionary who in his time set an example for revolutionaries today. He may be an apocalyptic visionary whose expectations proved mistaken. Or he may be the founder of the church, which through his Spirit is his living representative. (Even in this context there are many different views of the church's ethical authority.) He may also be regarded as a historical figure about whom almost nothing is known apart from his death on a cross. I mention these many ways of understanding Christ, not because I believe that they are all equally defensible, but in order to make it clear that to announce that the primary source of guidance for Christian ethics is the Biblical revelation with Christ as the center only begins the discussion. I shall not try to answer directly all the questions it raises, but I shall project a general view of how we should respond today to the Biblical source and of how that is related to other sources.

In the next chapter I shall call attention to two other distinctively Christian sources of ethical guidance: actual ethical learning that has taken place in the experience of the church, and contemporary learning that arises from ecumenical experience today.

There is continuous interaction between contemporary Christians and the Biblical sources. Our present experience shapes our response to those sources, and this present experience includes relevant knowledge of all kinds about the Bible itself, about ourselves, about the situations today in which we must act. There are shocks from events that open our minds to new questions and eliminate old answers. For example, successive shocks have come from the fact that most neglected and exploited people in the world are now able to speak to and push and sometimes displace those who have previously held most of the world's power and privilege. So far as Christian social ethics is concerned, this may be the most important fact of our time. It has destroyed the old paternalistic ethical answers based on the domination of most of the world by white men in the northern hemisphere. We read our Bibles differently because on all sides we encounter this new reality.

I have used the word "interaction" in speaking of this encounter with the Biblical sources, and it is a two-way street. The questions that we ask of the sources and many things that we emphasize as we seek answers come in large part from contemporary experience. But the Biblical events and personalities and teachings, the person of Jesus Christ himself, continue to have their influence on us even as we ask the questions. Biblical scholarship that helps us to understand the Biblical sources in their own context, that helps to develop in us historical empathy as well as contemporary concerns, makes a great contribution to our ethical thinking. Such scholarship, however, is inevitably colored by the present stance of the scholars as persons of our time. Openness to the effects of what is given historically may still modify that present stance. Varieties of present stances and freedom of historical criticism help to keep the interaction a two-way street.

THE TEACHING AND EXAMPLE OF JESUS

One issue that is central to Christian ethics is the extent to which we know about the example and the teachings of Jesus and how important whatever knowledge we have is thought to be. This is partly a historical question. It has also been treated as a question of theological priorities. Thus some theologians during the period of "neo-orthodoxy" made light of Jesus as a historical figure in contrast to the doctrines about Jesus Christ as the redeemer.

As one who is not a Biblical scholar I hope that I have

learned something from living through at least three periods of the struggles of Biblical scholars with the historical question. I have tried to learn from scholars as different as C. H. Dodd, my first teacher in the New Testament, who took a generally affirmative attitude toward the historicity of the Gospels, and Rudolf Bultmann, who has raised the most radical questions about that historicity.

In the first period there was the greatest possible emphasis, both in terms of historical confidence and in terms of theological priorities, on Jesus as a historical figure and on his teachings. This was an essential source of ethical authority and guidance for Walter Rauschenbusch and other social gospel writers. Liberal theologians influenced by Albrecht Ritschl supported this emphasis.

The second period, which combined historical skepticism with a strange theological indifference to the historical records about Jesus, began in this country as a result of earlier European influences with the rise of "neo-orthodoxy" in the 1930's and continued until the late 1950's. The kerygma, which was the proclamation of the redemptive meaning of the cross and the resurrection, became central, and the life and teachings recorded in the Synoptic Gospels became secondary. In British theology this tendency seldom went the whole way, but American New Testament scholars often reflected a high degree of historical skepticism. Reinhold Niebuhr, who never fitted stereotypes of neo-orthodoxy, though he is generally regarded as one of the most influential theologians of that second period, did not share either a centrally skeptical view of the Gospels or the neo-orthodox neglect of the historical Jesus. He said: "The Cross could not have the symbolic significance for Christian faith if the life and the doctrine were not consistent with it."[1] Paul Tillich, who was concerned to keep his essential message from being dependent on the inevitable uncertainties of historical fact, helped to convey the skeptical approach to the historical Jesus. Yet he made much of the "picture" of Jesus in the Gospels and, when pressed by students, would at times go quite far in conceding that he believed that "the picture" had a historical basis.

Today we are living in a period that is quite different from the second period—i.e., that of the dominance of skepticism and theological indifference to the historical Jesus. The view of Niebuhr, just quoted, regarding the importance of Jesus' life and doctrine, was similar to a concern of interpreters of the Gospels in the tradition of "form criticism" who came to speak of the "new quest" for the historical Jesus. They sought to find continuity between the kerygma and aspects of the personality and teachings of Jesus. In the school of Bultmann new efforts were made to offer a fuller historical portrait of Jesus, e.g., Günther Bornkamm's *Jesus of Nazareth*.[2]

It is a reflection of contemporary interests that the debate has begun again (there had been such a debate in the 1920's) as to whether or not Jesus was a political revolutionary. Now this issue is discussed by Biblical scholars as well as by those whose interests are primarily ethical or political. I shall say more about it later, but here I find it significant that particular questions about the teachings and example of Jesus are being debated, rather than the more general questions of the degree of our historical knowledge of Jesus and its theological importance.

In this third period a larger place is given to the teachings and example of the Jesus of the Gospels than was the case in the second period. The fact that it is later does not make it correct, but I think that one gains some advantage in perspective from the testing of the one-sided emphases of the two previous periods. I do not think that we will return to the first period, for today it is realized on all sides that there can be no biography of Jesus. The most that we can expect are glimpses of Jesus in action that often cohere with each other, and a body of teaching. We now realize better than the liberals of a generation or two ago—who found it easy to reconstruct the "Jesus of history"—that the Gospels share the

post-resurrection standpoint of the epistles. In the broad
sense of the idea of kerygma, involving a proclamation based
upon a response of faith, they are kerygmatic. W. D. Davies,
whose own great stature as a scholar is beyond dispute, has
consistently adhered to an affirmative rather than a skeptical
view about the historical records concerning Jesus. He has
summarized helpfully the more affirmative position of "the
Form Critics who belong to the post-Bultmannian period" in
the following passage:

> They do not consider that the new quest is the same
> as the quest of an earlier period; they do not consider
> that a full life of Jesus is possible. But they do recognize
> that the Jesus of History is essential to the preaching of
> the New Testament, and that it is possible through his
> words and deeds to grasp how Jesus understood himself
> and thus to find through his self-understanding a way to
> our self-understanding. Thus it is that, at a time when it
> seemed that the figure of Jesus was being still further
> hidden from us behind the interpretation, this time by
> the Gospel writers themselves, he has almost suddenly
> emerged from the dust of scholarship, and again oc-
> cupied the foreground of the New Testament.[3]

I believe that on the level of the deepest and most comprehensive ethical teaching there is a remarkable unity in the
New Testament. In Gospels and epistles, in the teachings of
Jesus recorded in the Synoptic Gospels, in the thought of
Paul and John and the Epistle of James, there is the same
emphasis on the supremacy of self-giving love. It is a love that
does not count the cost to self and finds the neighbor in every
person whom one meets or who is affected by what one does
or leaves undone. Such love is seen as the content of the
radical ethic of obedience to God as revealed in Christ. The
moment we seek to relate that radical ethic to complicated
social and political issues, many theoretical and practical issues emerge, and this book as a whole is about them.

GUIDELINES FOR INTERPRETATION

I shall now suggest some guidelines for the interpretation of the Biblical source of Christian ethics. I realize that it may seem presumptuous for one who is in no sense a Biblical scholar to do this. The difficulty is that the issues involved transcend Biblical scholarship; they are also in the province of the theologian, and of those who work chiefly in Christian ethics. The best that I can do is to project these guidelines and hope that others will test them in the light of their forms of expertise.

1. We should read the Bible with Christ as the center and the norm.

I have already referred to this principle and have indicated some of the difficulties that it raises. Yet, as a place to start, it does deliver Christians from the indiscriminate use of proof texts from anywhere in the Bible to justify what they may choose to do. If one admits the importance of the example and teaching of Jesus along the lines I have indicated, we have in them at least the source of norms for understanding the many interpretations of Jesus. The words that I have quoted from Reinhold Niebuhr seem to me to represent undeniable truth: "The Cross could not have the symbolic significance for Christian faith if the life and the doctrine were not consistent with it." The one who died on the cross was not an *x*, an otherwise unknown human being who was an agent of salvation. There is consistency between the spirit of Christ that comes to us through the epistles—for example, through I Cor., ch. 13, Rom., ch. 12, and Phil., ch. 2, to mention only a few passages—with the spirit of Christ that comes to us through the Synoptic Gospels. When Paul says: "Have this mind among yourselves, which you have in Christ Jesus," he has already sketched aspects of this mind that fit the picture of Jesus in the Gospels, and he projects this mind onto the drama of the incarnation that reflects the same spirit. Paul, whose epistles are the earliest testimony to the phenomenon of Jesus Christ as a historical reality, says at least that the death of Jesus was the consequence of his obedience. This means that it was neither a meaningless accident nor the result of a self-centered quest for martyrdom.

Given even a minimum knowledge of the content of the teachings of Jesus and of the quality of his life as an example, we can reject a great deal that has been done by Christians and defended on the basis of Biblical authority. Of all the cases of the ethical misuse of the Bible there can hardly be a worse one than its use to defend slavery in this country. H. Shelton Smith's book *In His Image, But . . .*[4] documents thoroughly this appalling story in the history of Christian ethics. He shows how this same use of the Bible continued to provide support for white racism long after the end of slavery.

One of the early antislavery prophets, John Woolman, the Quaker mystic (1720–1772) who carried on a continuous campaign against slavery in the American colonies, gives us an extraordinarily good example of the use of the Bible with a sense of its having a normative center. He was riding one day with fellow Quakers who began to talk in support of the slave trade. One did so by quoting the usual Biblical texts, claiming that Negroes were "the offspring of Cain, their Blackness being the mark which God set upon him after he murdered Abel." Another said that Ham belonged to Cain's race and he was sentenced to be a "servant of servants to his brethren." Woolman at first argued with them on their own terms and said that the flood had destroyed the whole outfit, that "all flesh died that moved upon the earth" (Gen. 7:21). And then, after appealing to a deeper level of Scripture saying that "the prophets repeatedly declare 'that the sons shall not suffer for the iniquity of the father, but everyone be answerable for his own sins,' " Woolman lashed out against them in terms of what was central to him in the Bible. The following passage is a good start on a theology of liberation:

The love of ease and gain are the motives in general of keeping slaves, and men are wont to take hold of weak arguments to support a cause which is unreasonable. I have no interest on either side, save only the interest which I desire to have the truth. I believe liberty is their [the slaves'] right, and as I see they are not only deprived of it, but treated in other respects with inhumanity in many places, I believe He who is a refuge of the oppressed will, in his own time, plead their cause, and happy will it be for such as walk in uprightness before him.[5]

This was an intuitive use of Scripture by one not versed in Biblical scholarship. He was able to cut through the false traditions based upon a few passages of Scripture, and there is no Biblical scholar who would deny that Woolman was right. It seems to me to be a model for the ethical interpretation of the Bible. I often reflect on the grim fact that the use of Biblical arguments to defend slavery did not come to an end until slavery itself was abolished. Must the Bible be used to defend an interest until events have destroyed it?

I had an experience during a visit in Bali, Indonesia, in 1971 that illustrates another common misuse of the Bible. In 1965 there was a coup in Indonesia that overthrew Sukarno and was regarded as a preventive action against an expected Communist coup. In a few weeks about four hundred thousand persons were massacred, 200,000 in Bali alone, an island of only 2,000,000 inhabitants. The victims were either Communists or suspected Communists or framed as such by neighbors. I visited a young pastor who told about his experience during those terrible days. He resolved to keep the people in his church from taking part in the killing. He found that some other ministers did not agree with him. One of them quoted Samuel's charge to Saul about slaying all the Amalekites and their cattle (I Sam. 15:3). Another referred to the story of Peter using the sword to cut off the ear of the high priest's servant, whose name was Malchus (John 18:10). The young pastor took the other side. He argued with these men by emphasizing the teaching of Jesus about love of neighbors, including enemies. He later reported that his own people who were persuaded by this point of view did not take part in the killing, but instead helped to protect people. There is a great deal in this episode. The use of Biblical texts to defend holy wars, which may become total wars such as the war against the Amalekites, has been another very common case of the ethical misuse of the Bible.

The United Presbyterian Church has given a good example to churches in its Confession of 1967, a new confession of faith that gives expression, among other things, to the concern of Christians for justice and peace in our time. The following principle is laid down, one that is in accord with the guidelines in this chapter: "The Bible is to be interpreted in the light of its witness to God's work of reconciliation in Christ." It emphasizes reconciliation between God and humanity, and this is integrally related to reconciliation in society between nations and races. The confession carries far this movement from Biblical teaching to social ethics and in doing so makes use of the example and teachings of Jesus. It says: "Because Jesus identified himself with the needy and exploited, the cause of the world's poor is the cause of his disciples." This is a good example of something that I shall have occasion to emphasize later: carefully planned corporate thinking about Christian ethics within an important unit of the church.

2. *The continuity between Jesus Christ and the Old Testament prophets should be emphasized.*

Without the Old Testament the New Testament can be read as a book of private religion or of religion involving responsibilities limited to the internal life of the church, even though these approaches are distortions. It makes a great difference if the New Testament is read together with the Old Testament. It is significant that the Gospel of Luke includes the Magnificat. This is not characteristic of the New

Testament, but the author of the Gospel must have sensed some appropriateness in including it. One wonders what Christians who had great power and privilege thought when they read or heard in church the familiar words:

> He has put down the mighty from their thrones,
> and exalted those of low degree;
> he has filled the hungry with good things,
> and the rich he has sent empty away.
>
> (Luke 1:52–53)

In medieval and modern times Roman Catholics were protected from the impact of those words so long as they were said or sung in Latin. There is a fascinating new use of them when Pope Paul refers to them to show that Mary really had the spirit of an activistic modern woman and represented a gospel of liberation.[6]

One of the passages in the Gospels most quoted in recent years is Jesus' own citation from Isa., ch. 61, in his address in the synagogue in Nazareth (Luke 4:18–19):

> "The Spirit of the Lord is upon me,
> because he has anointed me to preach good news
>   to the poor.
> He has sent me to proclaim release to the captives
> and recovering of sight to the blind,
> to set at liberty those who are oppressed,
> to proclaim the acceptable year of the Lord."

This passage, which the Evangelist puts at a crucial moment in the career of Jesus, links him directly with the prophets and with their concern for the victims of society.

There is no need here to summarize this aspect of the message of the prophets, but I shall quote one passage from their writings and the words of one modern interpreter.

I quote Jeremiah because he is not a prophet who is as much associated with this emphasis as, for example, Amos, and Isaiah of Jerusalem. He begins: "Woe to him who builds his house by unrighteousness, and his upper rooms by injus-

tice." Then he says to one of the corrupt sons of the good king
Josiah: "Do you think you are a king because you compete in
cedar? Did not your father eat and drink and do justice and
righteousness? Then it was well with him. He judged the
cause of the poor and needy; then it was well. *Is this not to
know me? says the* LORD." (Jer. 22:13a, 15, 16.) Could we
have a better statement of the integral relation between the
concern of a radical social ethic and the center of personal
religion, the knowledge of God?

Abraham Heschel, the great contemporary Jewish
prophet, who died in 1972, in his book on *The Prophets*
expressed what is central in the prophetic message about
social justice to both Jews and Christians. He made use of the
concept of "the divine pathos" and says this about God: "The
idea of the divine pathos combining absolute self-lessness
with supreme concern for the poor and exploited can hardly
be regarded as the attribution [to God] of human characteris-
tics. Where is the man who is endowed with such characteris-
tics?" Then he surprises by his way of putting it: "God's
unconditional concern for justice is not an anthropomor-
phism. Rather man's concern for justice is a theomorphism."[7]

The question is being raised insistently as to whether Jesus
himself was a revolutionary, even a political revolutionary.
This is related to the emphasis on his continuity with the
prophets. As I have said, this question recurs periodically,
often in concert with revolutionary impulses in society. Radi-
cals and conservatives alike tend to make Jesus over in their
own image. The claim is now being made that Jesus was a
fellow traveler of the Zealots. The late S. G. F. Brandon of the
University of Manchester has powerfully presented this view
in his scholarly book *Jesus and the Zealots.*[8] In order to make
his case he has to regard the emphasis in the Gospels on
peacemaking and love for enemies as later additions to the
Gospel record to prove to the Roman authorities that Christians were no threat to them and thus to gain for themselves
greater toleration. The elimination of extensive passages of

the New Testament because they are inconsistent with a scholar's theory is a familiar practice, but this passes the point of credibility for me.

Oscar Cullmann in his *Jesus and the Revolutionaries*[9] answers Brandon and some of the German scholars who had influenced him. Cullmann had dealt with aspects of this subject earlier in *The State in the New Testament*.[10] In both books Cullmann says that Jesus was executed by the Romans because he was believed to be a Zealot, and he makes much of the fact that one of Jesus' disciples was a Zealot. Cullmann believes that Jesus resisted the Zealot positions, that his teaching about nonviolence and about love for enemies is authentic. Cullmann's main point is that there is indeed a profound radicalism in the example and teaching of Jesus, but that it was essentially nonpolitical. He sees it as an eschatological radicalism that gives us few clues for social or political action today though it has great meaning for the transformation of the individual. He stresses the expectation for an early coming of the Kingdom of God. "The universal revolution," he says, "remains reserved for the establishment of the Kingdom of God. But within the yet-existing social framework his disciple is already personally to apply in a radical way the norms of the coming Kingdom."[11]

The teacher of Christian ethics who is not a New Testament scholar is in a difficult position amidst the debates between scholars. He has no recourse except to choose between them and in doing so to be guided by his own sense of what is real or important. As a matter of fact, I wonder if the differences between scholars on the deepest issues are not more influenced by their sense of what is real or important than by assured results of their scholarship. Otherwise how could they differ as much as Rudolf Bultmann and W. D. Davies do? I find Cullmann's main points more convincing than the view that Jesus was at heart an adherent of the cause of the Zealots. On the surface the substance of Cullmann's view is what I have always been taught. But I think that

Cullmann does concede something to the other side when he admits that Jesus had association with Zealots and that he was crucified as a Zealot revolutionary. He emphasizes the conviction that Jesus was more radical than the Zealots and that, while he expected no structural transformations of society until the coming of the Kingdom, this "does in no way detain Jesus from his work *in* this transitory world and *for* this transitory world."[12] Cullmann interpreted the work in personal rather than political terms.

I shall emphasize two aspects of the radicalism of Jesus that seem to me to be certain in spite of the confusion created by the debates between scholars. The first is that the career of Jesus—if we take seriously the many glimpses of his activities given in the Gospels—involved a series of public confrontations with various establishments. Consider the following examples. In his address in the synagogue in Nazareth he touched a very sensitive nerve within the group to which he was speaking by reminding his hearers that through Elijah and Elisha God had shown special favor to Gentiles—to the widow in Sidon, and to Naaman the Syrian. "When they heard this, all in the synagogue were filled with wrath. And they rose up and put him out of the city, and led him to the brow of the hill on which their city was built, that they might throw him down headlong." (Luke 4:28–29.) The author adds: "But passing through the midst of them he went away" (v. 30). Here Jesus radically challenged the racism (or ethnocentrism, or religious exclusivism) of the community.

Jesus confronted the religious establishment when on several occasions he healed on the Sabbath, putting compassion ahead of the law. He addressed his critics forthrightly: "I ask you, is it lawful on the sabbath to do good or to do harm, to save life or to kill?" (Mark 3:4). After he healed the man with the withered hand, these critics, who were labeled "Pharisees," "went out, and immediately held counsel with the Herodians against him, how to destroy him" (Mark 3:6). On another occasion he defended his disciples for plucking ears of corn on the Sabbath. This episode gave rise to one of the most liberating words in the New Testament: "The sabbath was made for man, not man for the sabbath" (Mark 2:27).

The same spirit of confrontation was present in his words that referred to Herod: "Go and tell that fox, 'Behold, I cast out demons and perform cures today and tomorrow, and the third day I finish my course" (Luke 13:32).

The most dramatic confrontation between Jesus and an establishment was his cleansing of the Temple. In this case he touched another sensitive nerve, the economic interest of the traders and money changers and of the political and economic forces behind them. I am not suggesting that Jesus was himself at this point concerned about economics. His outrage was directed against the defiling of the Temple as the house of God. But that did not alter the fact that economic interests were threatened. There is a close parallel between what Jesus did in the Temple, when "he would not allow anyone to use the temple court as a thoroughfare for carrying goods" (Mark 11:16, NEB), and recent demonstrations and moderate disruptions connected with protests against the war in Indochina. The acts of the Berrigans and their friends in destroying draft files seem quite similar to this event in two respects. There was a limited use of force, which was not intended to injure persons, though it did some damage to property. We have in the Temple episode no action that could provide an example for the use of lethal force, though we do have a departure from absolute nonresistance. Also, these examples of confrontation were not intended to solve social problems. They were symbolic actions that dramatized problems. In the case of the cleansing of the Temple, we may guess that the traders and the money changers were back in the Temple the next day. Similarly the destruction of draft files only slightly impeded the operations of the draft and of the military machine.

This pattern of active and resolute confrontation with establishments does give support to public activism under a great variety of circumstances. While it does not set an example of any particular form of political action, it is certainly far removed from a spirit of passivity or detachment or neutrality or privatism in relation to public issues. It also raises questions about the meaning of the saying about not resisting evil (Matt. 5:39). This teaching may best be understood from the context as forbidding retaliation against persons. Reinhold Niebuhr used this saying about nonresistance to undercut the tendency to find in Jesus support for nonviolent resistance.

I doubt if we can use a text to establish a law of nonviolence for all conceivable circumstances. But I think that we can say that in the Gospels there is strong prima facie support for the rejection of violence that puts the burden of proof on those Christians who believe they are justified in using it. And it is equally clear to me that there is no law favoring absolute nonresistance that would be consistent with the activity of Jesus himself.

The cumulative effect of these encounters brought Jesus to his death. The cross should not be seen only as the event that mediates the forgiveness of God to individuals and thus as the subject of theories of the atonement. It should also be seen as a historical event, the one event in the records about Jesus that is admitted to be historical by even the most skeptical scholars. As an event it tests the depth of the commitment of Jesus, and as an event it shows forth the suffering that can often be expected to be the consequence of obedience. Writers who have benefited from theology as a profession must often wince as they say such things. I know I do. This is especially true when we are aware of the sufferings today that have come to those who in their obedience have resisted cruel and oppressive powers in their nations. As an event the cross reminds us of the costly confrontations with similar powers that characterized the life of Jesus.

This has been the theme of much preaching and theological writing influenced by the social gospel. Walter Rauschen-

busch in his *A Theology for the Social Gospel* reinterpreted
the atonement. He suggested that Jesus died as a result of
collective sins that were similar to those in which we participate today. He enumerated six such sins as follows: religious
bigotry, the combination of graft and political power, the
corruption of justice, mob spirit and mob action, militarism,
class contempt. Under the last he included the whole pattern
of economic injustice and also the fact so generally experienced today that members of the lower economic classes
receive the cruelest punishments. Here Rauschenbusch
could have had racism in his scheme. He is often criticized
today for not having seen the blight of racism in society. In
other respects we might want to add to his list of collective
sins. In summarizing his view, he writes as follows: "Jesus
bore these sins in no legal or artificial sense, but in their
impact on his own body and soul. He had not contributed to
them, as we have, and yet they were laid on him. They were
not only the sins of Caiaphas, Pilate, or Judas, but the social
sin of all mankind, to which all who ever lived have contributed, and under which all who have ever lived have
suffered."[13] I am not suggesting that this is a full doctrine of
the cross, but it does bring out vividly one meaning of the
cross as it throws light on the life and work of Jesus in his own
time.

The second aspect of the attitudes and teachings of Jesus
that I want to emphasize is the extraordinary way in which
Jesus turns upside down the world's and the conventional
churches' classifications of people. To some extent this is seen
in an eschatological context referring to an age to come, as
in the Beatitudes, or in the story of the rich man and Lazarus,
or in the saying: "But many that are first will be last, and the
last first" (Matt. 19:30). Yet even sayings in that context have
meaning for the present. May we not say the same of such
a pronouncement as "Blessed are the meek, for they shall
inherit the earth"? (Matt. 5:5.) It is surely true of his saying:
"Truly I say to you, the tax collectors and the harlots go into

the kingdom of God before you" (Matt. 21:31).

There are many examples of this turning upside down of the conventional arrangement of people that need not be understood in terms of a futuristic eschatology at all. This is true of Jesus' preference of the publican or tax collector to the righteous Pharisee, of his preference of the prodigal son to the prudent elder brother, of his praise of the hated Samaritan in contrast to the honored priest and Levite. It is also true of his suggestion that little children perceive with a deeper wisdom than sophisticated adults, of his putting down of the rulers of Gentiles and of the usual conceptions of greatness in contrast to the role of servant. Note further his praise for the widow with her mite in comparison with the rich and their large contributions, his several statements about wealth as an obstacle to the true fulfillment of those who possess it. How can it be that his words about it being easier for a camel to go through the eye of a needle than for a rich man to enter the Kingdom of God (Mark 10:25) are taken so calmly in the churches of the northern hemisphere? Women who have a new consciousness of the way in which they have been treated as subordinate beings in both church and society, and who are repelled by the patriarchalism in so much of the Bible, find in Jesus one who did not discriminate against them.

This radical rearrangement of people may not always have political implications even in our time, but sometimes it does. This is especially true of the identification of Jesus with the poor, exploited, and neglected people, which I have already emphasized. Those who say that Jesus did not have in mind a political revolution or even a series of structural reforms on their behalf, even on behalf of slaves, are probably right. But this teaching does have radical political implications for us, especially in situations where the followers of Jesus have power and political leverage, where the church can influ-ence public opinion and from it can come pressures on governments and on centers of economic power. I do not believe that we can today deduce directly from the teaching of Jesus particular policies or legislation or ideological preferences about structures and strategies. But we do gain from his teaching a radical imperative to seek changes in structures and a sense of direction for the changes. We do learn from him priorities in a world shadowed by poverty and hunger, political terror and militarism. We learn to see the conflict between the institutions from which many of us profit and the demands implied in our faith. We should know that when followers of Jesus gather together they have political work to do that is a response to his teachings and to his mediation of the love of God for the people who are victims today.[14]

3. *The Bible should not be considered a book of laws that prescribe their own applications for all circumstances.*
There are broad and even radical imperatives such as those I have already stressed. At their center is the love commandment, with the understanding that the neighbors whom we are commanded to love are all persons affected by what we do or leave undone. Love in this context is not primarily a feeling, though it will be accompanied by feelings. Rather, it is a commitment, a responsibility. The full meaning of the contention that we cannot derive from this commandment or from Biblical teachings generally absolute laws will be clearer as I deal with concrete issues in later chapters. Here it may be enough to say that there are no specific directives concerning what we should do when one group of neighbors is in conflict with another, or when some neighbors oppress or exploit others. This is true when there is competition between the claims of those nearer neighbors for whom we may have special responsibility and distant neighbors whose needs may be greater. Such conflicts have produced profound dilemmas for Americans, and these will become more baffling in the years ahead. Though some forms of theology have encouraged too much of a double standard for what a person should do as an individual and

what he should do in a public office with its special responsibilities, there are also problems that do not yield to legalis-
tic solutions.

I do not regard "situationism" as being a self-sufficient
position in Christian ethics. But its proponents have demon-
strated the difficulty in dealing with choices in changing
situations in terms of absolute law. I believe that there are
strong moral pressures that put a heavy burden of proof on
those who make exceptions to what Joseph Fletcher admits
to be "generally valid" ethical norms.[15] These for Fletcher
can be more readily set aside for the sake of love than would
be consistent with what I call the burden of proof on those
who choose to set them aside. The moral pressure to avoid
the use of violence should be very strong even if it is not
absolute. I believe that there are moral limits which situa-
tionists do not theoretically recognize, and that there are
particular patterns of activity that should be regarded as
wrong under all conditions. For example, the torture that
dehumanizes and permanently injures persons, and that has
become the regular practice of many governments, is a hor-
rendous evil. So is the bombing of populations, which in the
Second World War and in the war in Indochina became
accepted policy on the part of the American Government. So
is its present policy of preparation for massive nuclear destruction of populations under certain conditions, which it
hopes to prevent by deterrence.

The danger of "situationism" in recognizing no limits in
principle to what is morally permissible can be well seen in
what is to me an extraordinary passage in Fletcher's *Situation Ethics*. He says that "on a vast scale of 'agapeic calculus'
President Truman made his decision about the A-bombs on
Hiroshima and Nagasaki."[16] If such a direct massacre of a
civilian population is consistent with *agape*, I fail to see that
there are any limits to the deeds of horror that can be permit-
ted in its name.

The reader may say that I have introduced negative laws

and in doing so I have not been consistent with the opening statement in this section about the Bible's not being a book of laws. Perhaps there is some truth in that criticism. Yet such negative laws as I may discover are not directly deduced from Biblical texts. Rather, they are forced upon one who has lived with the detestable results of particular patterns of decision and action. Decisions that lead toward such moral catastrophes as Auschwitz or Hiroshima are always wrong. In mentioning those two names in the same sentence I do not imply that the motives or the characters or the inner histories of the persons who made the decisions in those two cases were of the same moral quality. The contrast between the subjective dimensions of acts and their objective consequences can lead to moral confusion.

Take another type of illustration: the sayings of Jesus about divorce. These sayings carry important truth for us. They announce that permanence is an essential part of the intention of Christian marriage. In their own time they also called for the protection of women, who could be divorced at will by their husbands and who had no redress, and no hope for the future, when they were so victimized. I do not believe that out of these sayings of Jesus should be derived canon law prohibiting divorce today when a given marriage has been inwardly destroyed by long continued mutual hostility, and when women are not dependent upon marriage for status and support as they were in the first century. I also think that there are aspects of the nuclear family in our society that make the use of moral and religious law—not to speak of the law of the state—to preserve the marriage under all circumstances to be especially cruel and destructive.

4. *We should recognize the differences between our situation and that of Jesus and the New Testament writers.*
The people of the New Testament had no political power, no chance to influence public opinion in order to bring about structural changes in society. Also, they did not think in

terms of an indefinite future, but believed that God would bring history—as they knew it—to an end through the establishment of his Kingdom. How much the Kingdom was seen as involving the transformation by God of history on earth and how much it was regarded as a transcendental fulfillment beyond history may still be debated, but that issue is not important for this discussion. Planning for the future and long-term struggles for social changes were out of the question, as was the use of political power. It is understandable that Paul took for granted the institution of slavery and was content to encourage Christian masters and slaves to treat one another as Christian brothers and so in part to live as though there were no such institution. However, Paul's silence about slavery as an institution caused many American Christians as recently as the middle of the nineteenth century to teach that slavery was consistent with the teaching of the New Testament. This was based upon a terrible misunderstanding, and we should be warned by it concerning other matters that involve differences of possibility and responsibility between the first century and our own time.

In many countries today churches are in much the same situation in which the New Testament church found itself insofar as political power or freedom to act is concerned. Sometimes they are in worse situations because of the technological extension of governmental controls. Think of Paul's freedom of movement across boundaries and compare it with the restrictions on the movement of people today, especially those who have a reputation for encouraging dissent. It was said at Ephesus that "Paul with his propaganda has perverted crowds of people, not only at Ephesus but also in practically the whole of the province of Asia" (Acts 19:26, NEB). His chances today of obtaining a visa to visit many countries, including the United States, would be dim. However, in some countries, including the United States, Christians are not in a politically helpless position. It is possible for them to speak as citizens with great freedom and to organize for a wide range of public activities. They can seek to influence policies and to change institutions. Long-term struggles for justice and peace, for civil rights and liberties, are often an important part of their lives. Churches often provide for their support and channels for action.

We have periods of disillusionment, and today there are many who are tempted to give up on politics and on all public efforts to change structures. I can easily imagine the appearance of new movements for change and of new possibilities of political choice that would cause this mood to pass. But there is one serious source of political inhibitions among Christians that often makes them rather passive about political issues. They can read the New Testament without seeing that it has implications for public life. They find it natural to be preoccupied with private life, with the inner change of individuals, and with paternalistic expressions of love that raise no questions about structures or about the distribution of power. If they do understand the effect of structures on persons, and if they realize that their situation is different from that of the people of the New Testament, they should see that their responsibilities also are different. Those of us who still have considerable freedom to speak and to act publicly have no excuse for adhering to a privatistic interpretation of Christianity.

We who live under relatively free conditions and who generally have the protection of law are often shamed by the courage of others who under repressive governments run great risks and may suffer imprisonment, torture, or death as they protest against the crimes of government and keep alive a vision of a more humane society.

III
Forms of Corporate Ethical Guidance

We have seen how the Biblical revelation with Christ as the center is the primary source of guidance for Christian ethics. A second source of guidance for social ethics today comes from the experience of churches during nearly two thousand years of history. I believe that there has been real corporate learning on the part of Christians and that this is now too much neglected by a generation that cares little about history. Sometimes this learning has been negative. It has enabled churches to recognize that some interpretations of social ethics are wrong. This can be said today without impugning the motives or integrity of those who in earlier generations were able to defend positions that now seem clearly indefensible.

SOME HISTORICAL EXAMPLES

I have already referred to the long time it took for churches to reject what today would be seen on all sides as the intolerable, demeaning, and dehumanizing system of slavery. Many Christians finally learned this lesson because events forced it on them. And with the end of slavery the effort to find Biblical or Christian justification for it also came to an end. In most parts of the church today the same is true of systems of imposed racial segregation. The use of Biblical or Christian arguments for imposed segregation in this country may continue in some localities, but this too has withered as a result of events. Even when prejudices and opinions remain, public justification of them is seen to be hopeless.

The most complete turnabout in Christian thinking of which I have knowledge is the change that has come over the centuries in regard to religious liberty for those whom churches believe to be in error. This issue does not involve many open questions for those who are likely to read this book. It is, however, a remarkable paradigm of the way in which the Christian mind changes, and for that reason I shall emphasize it. I cannot get over the fact that it took so many centuries for Christians and churches to come to a position about which they now are generally agreed and really believe to be in accord with the gospel—the same gospel to which their predecessors had been exposed for all those years.

Most Protestants did not become clear about the claims for religious liberty that were implied by their own faith until the eighteenth century. Vestiges of older ideas and practices remained in many situations until the twentieth century. It is well to be reminded that, after the year 1673, Roman Catholics did not get the right to hold public office in England until 1829 and that even Protestant non-conformists could not enter Oxford or Cambridge University until the 1850's. The history of the wars of religion, of the persecution of Protestants by Catholics, of Catholics by Protestants, and of Protestant minorities such as the Anabaptists and Quakers by other Protestants often makes me wonder how churches retained moral credibility at all.

Much is owed to the courageous pioneers of religious liberty among those Protestant minorities as well as to the influence of thinkers of the Enlightenment on the fringe of the church or outside it. Main-line Protestant churches came to accept religious liberty before Catholicism partly because they had less effective organs of authority with doctrinal support than Catholics. Perhaps even more it was because they more often lived in pluralistic situations and they were almost required by religious competition to accord religious liberty to fellow citizens, perhaps to business customers, of rival communions. Yet this came hard so long as there was the general assumption that the social unity of a nation was incompatible with the coexistence of opposing branches of the church in that nation. This was sincerely believed and it was undermined less by argument than by the painful experience of having to adjust to a religious pluralism that could not be rooted out.

Whatever the legal situation and however much religious liberty is accepted in principle, by both Protestants and Catholics, the social pressure of religious majorities on religious minorities in many situations continues to create forms of extralegal discrimination. Even in the United States legal discrimination is felt by some religious minorities—for example, by Jews in the commercial use of Saturday and Sunday.

As late as the 1950's Roman Catholics had not achieved a clear doctrinal basis for the support of religious liberty for all. However, there was the fact that Catholicism flourished in such countries as the United States where it had no legal privilege and where religious liberty for all was taken for granted. Here and in some other countries Catholic authorities developed a pragmatic acceptance of the coexistence of the Catholic church with other churches and of religious liberty both for all Christians and for those outside the Christian circle. John Courtney Murray in the 1950's was the major Catholic proponent in this country of religious liberty for all on principle and not merely as a pragmatic accommodation to the pluralistic situation. His own freedom to publish was curtailed by church authorities until about the time of the Second Vatican Council, where both his position on religious liberty and he himself were completely vindicated.

The Declaration on Religious Freedom of Vatican II was the final ratification of the principle of religious liberty for all. It came at the end of a long and very costly learning process.

And when it did come it was a great relief for both Catholics
and non-Catholics. It expressed what countless Catholics had
deeply believed for a long time, but at the top level the
church had never been able to clear its mind on the subject
of religious liberty in principle. In some cases (such as Spain
and Colombia, which I mention as extreme examples), the
denial of religious liberty by states with Catholic majorities
was most oppressive. I quote two paragraphs from the Declaration on Religious Freedom:

> This freedom means that all men are to be immune from
> coercion on the part of individuals or of social groups and
> of any human power, in such wise that in matters reli-
> gious no one is to be forced to act in a manner contrary
> to his own beliefs. Nor is anyone to be restrained from
> acting in accordance with his own beliefs, whether pri-
> vately or publicly, whether alone or in association with
> others, within due limits.
>
> The Synod further declares that the right to religious
> freedom has its foundation in the very dignity of the
> human person, as this dignity is known through the re-
> vealed Word of God and by reason itself. This right of the
> human person to religious freedom is to be recognized
> in the constitutional law whereby society is governed.
> Thus it is to become a civil right.

That declaration has proved to be more than words. It has
set in motion fundamental changes not only at the top in the
Catholic Church but even in countries where there had been
no religious liberty because of the church's former position
on this issue. Even Spain and Colombia began to change.
Together with other developments that have come from
Vatican II, especially from its recognition of the ecclesial
nature of Protestant churches, there has been a complete
change of climate in the relations between Catholics and
Protestants and between Catholics and the community as a
whole. Today in the United States the fear of Catholic power
that was so dominant in the 1950's has largely disappeared.

There was widespread fear in 1960 that a Catholic president would undermine the religious liberty of Americans. But only a few years later there was almost no anxiety among Protestants concerning the Catholicism of Eugene McCarthy, Robert Kennedy, or Edmund Muskie. John Kennedy proved that a Catholic layman was not necessarily controlled by the hierarchy, and this fact, together with the developments coming from Vatican II, contributed mightily to this amazing change.

The declaration on religious freedom made by Vatican II is a perfect example of recognition so late in the day of what is now believed to be known through the Word of God. This paradigm illustrates very well the need for continuous interaction between present experience and insight and the Biblical sources of ethical guidance.

Closely connected with the issue of religious liberty has come a widespread recognition of the moral and religious inadequacies of established churches, which are partly controlled by the state and which have special privileges granted by the state. This was part of the pattern of *Christendom* in both western and eastern Europe, and it may have been justified at one time. Now that the pattern has been broken it is increasingly recognized that close relations with the state are bad for the established church itself and incompatible with full freedom for members of other churches or for non-Christians in a pluralistic society. It is better for the church to be on its own than to have to depend upon the state. The state itself needs to be confronted by an independent church, and the church as a community is stimulated by the participation of its laity in its support and its governance.

The European establishments that still remain are under radical review, as for example in Sweden. The English establishment today is only possible because of the English genius for changing the substance of institutions while retaining many of the ancient forms and symbols. The English establishment is now precarious, and one thing can be said about it: it would be possible only in England. Even now a serious reconsideration is taking place with regard to one of the remaining forms of interference by the state in the governing of the Church of England, i.e., the appointment of bishops by representatives of the state.

There are disagreements on all sides in the churches about forms of government, but Christian sanction has been generally removed from despotisms. We are seeing the gradual death of the idea that under no circumstances should Christians resist tyrannical and oppressive political powers. Sometimes practical resistance as a live possibility is out of the question. But the confident use of doctrines of divine providence to support the divine right of kings or of any other rulers has disappeared. The modern experience with totalitarianism that has been hostile to churches and that has exceeded flagrantly the authority which rightly belongs to any state—both on issues of religion and on issues of justice —has been the last straw for most who have opposed all resistance to political authorities on theological grounds.

One of the most interesting chapters in the history of Christian political thought is the history of the exegesis of Rom. 13:1–7. No longer can this passage be invoked as a law that identifies disobedience to rulers with disobedience to God. Such a contention is likely to be countered with the words: "We must obey God rather than men" (Acts 5:29) or by reference to Rev., ch. 13. Sometimes it is simply rejected as time-bound, perhaps as a reflection of Paul's rather favorable experience of the Roman authorities, or as representing a wise strategy of the church in the first century—necessary if it was to secure toleration by the state. There have also been attempts to see in this passage criteria that limit the state's exercise of authority, such as the statement in Rom. 13:3 that "rulers are not a terror to good conduct, but to bad." This seems to suggest that Rom., ch. 13, does not apply to a malevolent tyranny, i.e., a government that is a terror to conduct which the church can only regard as good and that rewards conduct which the church can only regard as bad.[1]

Another approach has been to see Rom. 13:1–7 as part of a long passage that includes ch. 12 and also the verses that follow, beginning with ch. 13:8: "Owe no one anything, except to love one another; for he who loves his neighbor has fulfilled the law." Paul Lehmann has recently based his highly qualified justification of revolution on the conviction that the injunction to obey the governing authorities must always be seen as subordinate to love.

All of this loosening up of the Biblical basis for the strong traditional support for obedience to governments is an example of what I call learning from historical experience. One episode that illustrates the change that has come was the part that Dietrich Bonhoeffer played in the plot against Hitler. The decision to become engaged in that conspiracy and, along with it, to use his role deceptively in the military intelligence as a way of undermining the state was for him as a Lutheran extremely difficult.

The issue of whether or not resistance to political authorities is theologically permissible must be distinguished from the issue of the permissible use of violence in such resistance. Christians are divided in different ways on those two questions. But I doubt if many Christians with broad influence in the future will hold to a view that was very common in the past: i.e., that violence by political authorities in repressing their citizens is always justified because of the state's divinely sanctioned authority, but that revolutionary violence against a tyrannical state is always wrong.

My next example of ethical learning by the church in history has to do with the ethics of war. The prospect of nuclear war and of the possible annihilation of whole populations, perhaps of the human race itself, has given the prevention of war a place of much higher priority than ever before in the social ethics of churches. Vatican II summarized widespread Christian thinking in the following words: "Any act of war aimed indiscriminately at the destruction of entire cities or of extensive areas along with their population is a crime against God and man himself." Yet such an act of war will almost certainly be characteristic of a nuclear war. Even a limited, nonnuclear war may easily escalate to the point of nuclear war. The Uppsala Assembly of the World Council of Churches in 1968 through the report of one of its sections said that the prevention of nuclear war is the first duty of governments.

I shall have more to say in a later chapter about the war in Indochina. Here I shall emphasize one thing that has been learned from it. In the past the traditional view that there are "just wars" that a state may be right in waging has generally been supported by most churches. This view has been elaborated with most precision by Roman Catholic ethicists. The effect of it generally has been to show that any particular war in which a nation is engaged is just. Churches have usually supported the war effort of their own nations; they have taken for granted the justice of the causes for which they were fighting; and they have seldom questioned the justice of their mode of warfare. In the United States the war in Indochina brought about a reversal of this use of the conception of the just war. The criteria used to show that a war is just have been widely used by both Catholics and Protestants to show that the Indochina war was unjust, that the cause of the United States was unjust, and that its methods of fighting were unjust. This landmark in Christian thinking about war in this country has been given wide ecumenical support among churches in other countries. Surely there is good reason to believe that thinking about the ethics of war will never again reflect the complacent assumption that war is both an expected and a usually justified function of the state.

The church has also learned a great deal about the perils its social dominance held for its own integrity. As the dynamic religion that helped to create Western civilization, Christianity has itself suffered distortion in the process. Its adherents ended up on top of that civilization and from that vantage point came to dominate most of the earth. This should not be said in cynicism, because in some contexts it has been a sign of the success of Christianity in permeating civilization with its vision of reality and with some of its ideals. There have also been great moral, intellectual, and artistic achievements within Western civilization that it is not necessary to renounce. I have used the word "distortion" deliberately. It refers to the tendency to see the world and its institutions from the perspective of dominant nations and classes, and also from the perspective of white men. Dorothee Soelle, one of the strong new voices in theology, has put it this way: "The Christ who rules in the church and who has supplanted the biblical Christ is the Christ of the rulers."[2] Already I have suggested the practical meaning of this distortion as seen by Rauschenbusch, Cone, and Archbishop Câmara. Conservative interpretations of divine providence have given sanction to the dominant political and economic powers. The result is a strong tendency to translate Christian love into expressions of paternalism or a condescending philanthropy. This has involved at best an unconscious white racism and at worst religiously sanctioned but hateful race prejudice. It also involved the presumed right of the imperial powers, often with religious sanction, to carve up the earth and assume control over most of its inhabitants out of greed and vainglory. In the United States during the very years in which theologians in the South were justifying slavery, theologians in the North were teaching that the laws of *laissez faire* were laws of God and that deviations from them, such as the organizing of workers to raise their wages, were violations of those laws.

The bishops of the worldwide Anglican communion, meeting in the Lambeth Conference of 1948, in one of their reports said:

We have to admit that the Christian Church through the formative decades of the industrial era showed little insight into what was befalling human society. It was still thinking in terms of feudalism. The Church of England was identified almost completely with the ruling classes, as were the churches of central and eastern Europe. Its own economy had the marks of a dying feudalism or latterly of bourgeois society. Apart from provision for education of the poor and the work of some churchmen for the emancipation of slaves and of children in factories, it was slow to take the initiative in the desperate fight for social justice. A churchman here or there, a Christian group here or there wholeheartedly upheld the cause of the oppressed, but only in more recent times has the church begun to make a radical critique of Western society, and to provide a climate that is not hostile to revolutionary spirits.[3]

That statement is a remarkable testimony to the amount of learning that has taken place among responsible leaders of the church who were not extremists or ideologues. Doubtless they remembered with pain the Parliamentary Reform bill enacted in Britain in 1832. That bill, which began the process of extending the elective franchise to all the people, was passed by Parliament, but almost all the bishops in the House of Lords voted against it (their vote was 21–2). Between 1832 and 1948 a great deal of learning had taken place, and the same has been true of most churches. Churches that had been at the right hand of the old powers began to listen to their victims and their critics. Many of their leaders identified themselves morally and politically with the new forces that were struggling for justice and human rights. Today churches are still learning on a global scale that awareness of the distortion we have been discussing here must involve a radical change of perspective, a change of mind and heart.

My last example of a change in Christian thinking that has come belatedly is a change in attitudes toward the Jewish people. Of all the abominations that have had large-scale support by Christians and sanction in much traditional theological teaching there has been none greater than the anti-Judaism that inspired anti-Semitism and led to the political and social persecution of Jews. There are many other ingredients in anti-Semitism, but the Christian rejection of the Jewish people because they rejected Christ and were regarded as responsible for his death has been an important one. It has made a bias against Jews a part of the culture of Christendom. Given that bias, they have been a convenient scapegoat, and the ills of nations have often been traced to them. This continues to be the case but the defenses for it have lost respectability in churches.

The holocaust, the murder of six million Jews in gas chambers in the middle of Europe by the Nazis, has revealed the depths of evil in human history more horribly than any other event in modern times. It revealed the enormity of the cruelty implicit in the anti-Semitism that had been inspired in part by the anti-Judaism of Christians. The diagnosis of anti-Semitism is highly complicated and sometimes it is seen as a sign of a covert rejection of Christianity itself. This complicating paradox does not annul the historical responsibility of Christians for many of its manifestations. This reality has come to be taken seriously within the church. I realize that nothing that is done now can atone for the crimes of the past or fully remove the threat to themselves that Jews often find implicit in Christianity. I do not think that Reinhold Niebuhr overstated the matter in a famous passage in which he renounced the Christian missionary attempt to convert Jews. He says that "practically nothing can purify the symbol of Christ as the image of God in the imagination of the Jew from the taint with which ages of Christian oppression in the name of Christ tainted it." He adds: "This is not merely an historic matter. We are reminded daily of the penchant of anti-semitic and semi-fascist groups, claiming the name of Christ for campaigns of hatred."[4]

Charles Glock and his colleagues published two studies of the pervasive religious prejudice against Jews in the churches, one a study of the laity and the other a study of the clergy.[5] There are great differences between denominations and especially between those who tend toward a literalistic approach to the Bible and those who have assimilated critical Biblical studies. Yet the revelation of these investigations concerning the religious roots of anti-Semitism that are still present in the American Christian community is frightening. For example, members of the clergy were asked to respond to the following statement: "The Jews can never be forgiven for what they did to Jesus until they accept him as the true saviour." Across the board among nine Protestant denominations 48 percent said that they strongly disagreed, 27 percent said that they disagreed, 9 percent said that they strongly agreed, 10 percent said that they agreed, and 6 percent had no opinion. It is encouraging that 75 percent disagreed. But there is evidence of the depth of the problem in the past, and of its continued existence, in the fact that 19 percent agreed, and that 6 percent were indifferent. There is some sign of a steady movement away from this kind of thinking based on proof texts. Much better were the responses to the following statement: "The reason that the Jews have so much trouble is because God is punishing them for rejecting Jesus." In response to this only 8 percent are in the combined categories of "strongly agree" or "agree," with only 2 percent taking the former position; only 4 percent had no opinion. The shocking thing is that contemporary Jews are still held responsible by a considerable minority for what was done in the first century! It is also shocking that the same minority of Christians have in the back of their minds a picture of spiritually blackmailing Jews into conversion. The findings concerning lay attitudes are more disheartening than those about the clergy. I cite these studies partly to show that only a minority holds views of this kind. But I also think that such frank exposure of anti-Judaism in the churches has come to be an important lesson for Christians who have refused to believe that anti-Semitism has significant religious roots.

The New Delhi Assembly of the World Council of Churches in 1961 adopted a resolution that not only reaffirmed a resolution against anti-Semitism that had been adopted at the First Assembly in Amsterdam in 1948 but also added the following: "In Christian teaching the historic events which led to the Crucifixion should not be so presented as to fasten upon the Jewish people of today responsibilities which belong to our corporate humanity and not to one race or community. Jews were the first to accept Jesus and Jews are not the only ones who do not yet recognize him." In the same spirit Pope Pius XII and Pope John XXIII deleted words from the Good Friday liturgy that were derogatory in regard to the Jews.

The most dramatic facing of these issues has been in the Roman Catholic Church. The Second Vatican Council repudiated the idea of collective guilt for the death of Christ, the guilt of "all the Jews then living, without distinction," or of "the Jews of today." It is a sign of the depth of the problem in the past that Vatican II (as also the New Delhi Assembly) had to go out of its way to say that the Jews of today are not to be blamed. Vatican II, in its summarizing statement about anti-Semitism, said the following: "The Church repudiates all persecutions against any man. Moreover, mindful of her common patrimony with the Jews, and motivated by the gospel's spiritual love and by no political considerations, she deplores hatred, persecutions, and displays of anti-Semitism directed against the Jews at any time and from any source." Again, it says a lot about the past that the council had to say now that these outrages are deplored. This statement as a whole has elements in it that Jews could regard as patronizing and those familiar with the debates that preceded it could feel that it had been at some points watered down. But, taken as it is as a basis for policy it has already made a great difference in the attitudes of Christians toward Jews. And, most important, it will change what is taught about Jews in the context of Biblical events in Christian schools around the world.

The history of this matter is such that nothing that one says on this subject does justice to its enormities. But Christians have learned from the holocaust what the end result of some of their attitudes can be. They have also learned, from a very intensive reexamination of their own explicit teaching, of their own need to change.

I have mentioned a few examples of things learned by churches—or perhaps more accurately, within churches—on social ethics that should form important chapters in Christian social ethics. I doubt whether there are examples of more importance than those which I have chosen, though there are others of like importance. I hope that I have illustrated my point that we have in this historical experience a place to look for guidance for ethical decisions today.

Continuing Ecumenical Guidance

I shall now deal with the processes by which we should plan for better corporate guidance within the church now. I shall consider the substance of such guidance only incidentally as I give illustrations of the process.

Today there is a desirable emphasis on the grass roots, on participation by people at the local level, on local congregations. There is distrust of large organizations and especially of distant bureaucracies in New York, Geneva, or Rome. Denominations that have connectional or hierarchical structures are often characterized by a *de facto* congregationalism. There is much that is right in this tendency. Yet, on many of the more fateful issues, local or regional or even national units of the church are not self-sufficient. Local congregations are usually too homogeneous in race, social experience, and interests to see society as it is experienced by those whose social history and background are markedly different. Even on local issues a larger unit than the congregation is needed, a unit that includes inner city and suburb and varied racial or ethnic groups. Many of our most baffling social problems are global, and this is a globe that is pro-

foundly affected by decisions of American citizens. Members
of American churches need to see how these decisions appear to people in other countries. Ideally, local churches
should have their windows open and winds from the worldwide Christian community should blow through them. I fear
that more often than not their windows are almost closed.
Their tendency toward self-containment causes them to be
uncritical of the cultural, social, or national outlook that con-
tinuously forms the minds of their members.

There is a common tendency today to downgrade the
larger organizations of the church. This is natural because
they seem remote. They appear to have too much power of
initiative, and in the nature of the case the number of persons
who can have the experience of direct participation in them
is extremely limited. I hear such phrases as "eastern
ecumenical establishment," "social action curia," "unity
from the top down," "an ecclesiastical elite." If there is to be
meeting in the flesh between people from the grass roots in
many places, there has to be a modest bureaucracy and costly
air travel is necessary. The latter obviously limits the numbers that participate, and the raising of the needed funds
requires organization. Ecumenical organizations provide
necessary structures for a worldwide Christian community
that is already a reality. The test of such organizations is the
degree to which they enable persons at the grass roots in one
part of the world to be aware of the experience of those at
the grass roots in another part of the world, of their needs,
their sufferings, their aspirations, their convictions. Emphasis
on the grass roots is an essential corrective of an abstract
ecumenicity. But there can soon be too much emphasis on
isolated grass roots.

One of the greatest changes to come about in the church
in my lifetime is the new relationship between Protestants
and Catholics. Both have had their visions of the church
greatly enlarged because now without reserve they include
each other in those visions. Even on the local level their new

relations broaden the base of the Christian community to a remarkable degree. Protestants are stimulated by Catholic thought as well as by such phenomena as Catholic Pentecostalism on the one hand and Catholic social activism on the other. One contribution of Catholicism that helps to overcome local provincialism is the presence of religious orders of men and women, which have considerable freedom from local church authorities and which are much influenced by their presence in varied social situations and in many countries. As an example of this, I have been made sensitive to much that is happening in Latin America by Jesuits with whom I work who are oriented toward Peru, Chile, Guatemala, and other Latin-American countries.

Polls of members of churches at the grass roots, registering their first and unexamined opinions on controversial issues, often reveal that opinions in churches differ little, if at all, from prevailing opinions in the strata of society most represented among them. Such polls concerning issues of race or of foreign policy or of economic justice often make one wonder if Christian teachings about social ethics have any effect at all within the churches. There need to be processes by which those first and unexamined expressions of opinion are tested and sifted. They need to be examined in the light of theological and ethical criticism and in exchanges of conviction between suburb and ghetto dwellers, between those who live in nations that find the *status quo* so favorable that they resist all changes and those who live where people are inclined to believe that almost any change would be an improvement.

I shall give one controversial illustration from the recent history of my own denomination, the United Church of Christ. Several years ago the denomination's Council for Christian Social Action prepared a statement calling for amnesty for war resisters to be submitted for approval to the General Synod, the denomination's highest judicatory. This statement was sent to local churches for their criticisms. Insofar as they responded, they were three to one against amnesty, but most did not respond at all and so this result was inconclusive. When the General Synod met in the summer of 1968, a rather early date as we may think now for amnesty to have a chance for approval, there was an extensive debate on the subject. As a result the Synod voted four to one in favor of amnesty. One could regard that as an example of how the local units of the church can be betrayed by the larger units. Or one could regard that experience as an example of the way the church changes its mind, or minds change in the church. The first and unexamined expressions of opinion are likely to be influenced by conventional views of patriotism unaffected by the church's own message. But when the issues are discussed in a different setting in which theological and ethical illumination does take place, in which conventional views are challenged by those who represent quite different outlooks, it is understandable that the case for amnesty gains wider support. Amnesty is seen both as a delayed response to the consciences of many war resisters and as an act of reconciliation. I think that each case of this sort has to be judged on its merits and the testing of what has taken place should continue. It is only an episode in a process.

I used as an illustration the action of the United Church's General Synod, but not in order to emphasize the ecclesiastical authority of that body—for in fact it can do no more than recommend to the churches that make up the denomination. My purpose was, rather, to call attention to the action of a representative group of church members who happened to be together.

Today many Roman Catholics have the same problem that Protestants have in determining which teaching of the church carries moral authority for them. Pope Paul VI has issued two famous encyclicals: *Populorum Progressio*, which deals with problems of justice between rich and poor nations and the problems of development in the poor nations, and *Humanae Vitae*, which proclaims once more the traditional teaching against the use of contraceptives. Encyclicals as such are not believed to be infallible, but they do have great weight. Many Catholics find intrinsic authority for matters of justice in *Populorum Progressio* but reject the teachings about contraceptives set forth in *Humanae Vitae*. Indeed seven hundred American Roman Catholic theologians signed a statement opposing the teaching of the latter encyclical. This is an amazing development. There is another interesting fact about *Humanae Vitae*. The pope had appointed a large commission, including medical doctors, and moral theologians, and bishops, to advise him on the subject of birth control. There were even lay men and women on it. The commission by a large majority endorsed a report calling for a change in the teaching and policy of the church concerning contraceptives, but the pope took his stand with a small minority of the commission. Since both the majority and the minority reports were published in the press, Catholics have been able to compare the report of experts, which has considerable intrinsic authority, with the encyclical, which has behind it the authority of a magisterial fiat. Pope Paul may well have thought that in refusing to change the teaching of his predecessors he was shoring up papal authority, but in all probability he was undermining its credibility. I predict that one of his successors will have to yield on this subject, because both the experience of the laity and the teaching of the theologians are to so large an extent on the other side.

One form of corporate guidance in the ecumenical community seems to me to have great value. Some agency of the church officially calls together a group of persons who are then asked to give systematic consideration to a major social issue and to speak for themselves unofficially to the churches, or in some instances to the nation. There has been a great deal of experience with this type of operation. It has some advantage over statements by judicatories that meet primarily for other purposes, though judgments by such bodies are at times desirable, for their silence may in practice be a message of apathy or a message of consent to the *status quo*. The group that is called to speak for itself has the advantage of being better able to break new ground, and it can have considerable weight.

One of the best illustrations of this process was the World Conference on Church and Society that met at Geneva in July 1966. It was officially called by the World Council of Churches and was supported by funds raised by the World Council and made possible also by the work of the Council's staff. It was charged to speak to the Council and through it to the churches. It was made up of somewhat more than four hundred persons, most of whom were delegates representing churches. Its work was based upon several years of preparation that resulted in the publication of four substantial volumes on the issues with which the conference was to deal. One of the most important facts about this conference is that nearly half of the members came from the churches of Asia, Africa, and Latin America. It therefore could not have been said to represent proportionately the membership of the churches of all continents, but it was able to bring the needs and anxieties and aspirations of the Third World to the attention of the churches of Europe and North America to an extent that had never been the case before. It dealt with the problems of development, of political structures in new nations, of revolution, of war and peace, of apartheid, of rapid technological and cultural changes and much more. The main concerns of this unofficial conference were given strong support by the Fourth Assembly of the World Council of Churches, its official decision-making body, meeting in Uppsala in 1968. Since that time the World Council has been a sounding board for the people of the Third World. Another fact about the Geneva Conference is that half the delegates were lay men and women and many of these were politicians and economic experts. I shall attempt to convey some sense of its effect on those who attended it by quoting from the report of an American delegate, a Presbyterian banker from

Philadelphia. I think that what he says about his response suggests more vividly than anything that I could say in general terms about the deeper levels of corporate guidance that such a meeting makes possible. He wrote as follows:

> Before going to the Conference two statements were made to me by friends who had had previous experience in World Council affairs. Here was one of them: "As an American, and especially as an American businessman, you will have a new kind of experience engaging in discussion with dedicated Christians from many parts of the world who *do not share your assumptions.*" This turned out to be the understatement of the year. The experience was not only new, it was traumatic. . . . For the first several days I churned. The other friend made this statement: "I am sure of one thing, Bob. You will go as a Christian, but you'll come back a much better one." He was absolutely right.
>
> The greatest achievement of the Conference was that it didn't break up. It could have. Only the cohesive force of Christian love held it together. At no time in my life have I ever witnessed so clearly the tremendous power of that love. During those two weeks of long and grueling hours each day (and this was my vacation!), I came closer to understanding what Jesus meant when he said that it isn't enough to love our friends; even the Pharisees do that. We were told by our Lord that we had to love our enemies. I sure felt at times that I had encountered some enemies—or, as the saying goes, if these are my friends, who needs enemies?
>
> However, it gradually dawned on me that I was not alone in undergoing trial, you see; for many of the others, *I was the enemy.* I had never quite thought of myself in that light. My prayers began to take a new turn. I asked not only that I be given the will and the power to love my enemies, but that my enemies be given the will and power *to love me.* I think we did make great strides in coming to love one another in the *agape* sense, which doesn't mean we had to agree with each other's views.[6]

The Geneva Conference created a great deal of discussion in this country partly because Paul Ramsey, who was present, wrote a serious criticism of it in a book entitled *Who Speaks for the Church?* [7] He felt that it was unrepresentative of the constituency of the churches; that many of its recommendations to policymakers might lead to consequences for which those who made them would not want to take responsibility, but with which the policymakers would have to live; and that far too much was decided on too many subjects in too short a time. He did admit that he could say "without hesitation that the caliber of the reports was astonishingly good." [8] He called attention to the fact that while there were experts and politicians present, the latter were mostly legislators and there were few people responsible for policymaking. His criticism of the conference was directed against its methodology more than against particular conclusions. Much of the emotion behind the book was his resentment against the conference's condemnation of the American military presence in Vietnam and "the long continued bombing of villages in the south and of targets a few miles from cities in the north." He said that this was the most "newsworthy conclusion of the conference." [9] He was critical of the fact that most of the Americans present, including myself, strongly supported this condemnation of American policy. For this reason he could say that they did not represent their own churches, and this was certainly true in 1966. Ramsey's criticisms of the reports should be taken seriously, as there is no more acute mind working on these issues. I believe that he is wrong in his rejection of the process, for it was not intended to represent the constituencies but to give special attention to the problems of the Third World. To limit what is said at such a time to what people in the churches already think would cut the church off from very important stimuli and guidance. On the issue of the war in Vietnam it is difficult for me not to see what was said in Geneva in 1966 as prophetic of what came to be commonplace in the churches of this country by 1970. The title of Ramsey's book, *Who Speaks for the Church?* begins at the wrong point. Anyone who speaks *for* the church will have little that is fresh to say on new issues. I should emphasize the need to plan for a variety of forms of speaking *in* the church which would also in many situations be speaking *to* the church.

A second illustration is the Cleveland Conference on World Order that was called by the National Council of Churches in 1958 and charged to speak for itself to the churches. It became known for its calling for steps by our Government toward the recognition of mainland China. This created a great furor at the time. The National Council and also denominations that belonged to it were relentlessly attacked. I have a considerable file of the attacks made on me because of my part in the drafting of its most controversial statement. The idea of recognizing Communist China in 1958 was almost a case of thinking the unthinkable. The furor continued for several years, though gradually public opinion began to change on the subject and in 1972 President Nixon was given great credit because of his visit to Peking. I am sure that in 1958 no one could have been more shocked by the action of the Cleveland conference than Richard Nixon. There is no way of measuring the long-term effect of that action on the churches and on the nation, but it would be strange if it were not seen as helping to break the ice on a most feared subject and helping to prepare for the changing of public opinion that came eventually. If nothing had been said except that which would have been regarded as representative of the churches, there would have been a real loss.

A third example, which is in some respects similar, comes from the experience of the church in the Federal Republic of Germany. In 1965 a group of influential clergy and lay persons on their own initiative prepared a memorandum on the question of the lost provinces of Germany and the question of its eastern boundary. There were at least eleven million refugees in West Germany from those provinces at the time, and in principle many of them hoped to return home. The government had been wise in its relocating of the refugees, and the economy was prosperous. These factors made it possible for them to be assimilated, and therefore the problem created by their being refugees was more manageable than would otherwise have been the case. This issue at that time was as much taboo as the discussion of recognizing Communist China had been in this country in 1958. This memorandum raised the question of German reconsideration of the whole matter of the eastern boundary. It did not prescribe a solution but asked to have a certain position (one that had been assumed to be the only patriotic German position) reexamined with an open mind. The memorandum was originally unofficial, but it was later given official status by the Federation of the German Evangelical Church (E.K.i.D.). In 1965 there was also a great furor because churchmen had dared to speak out in this way on so controversial an issue. It could be seen more readily within the church than in the nation as a whole that Germany had brought upon herself this loss of her provinces by her own aggression. Moreover, it was clear that there could be no peace in Europe for the indefinite future if Germany remained intent on recovering those territories as, for example, France had remained intent on recovering Alsace-Lorraine after its loss in 1871. What was only suggested by the church in 1965 became the policy of the government of Chancellor Willy Brandt in 1972. Again it would be strange if the church had not helped to break the ice in connection with this most difficult political issue. I think that we have in this case an excellent example of how corporate thinking within the church provides ethical guidance not only to members of the church but also to the nation.

Today the World Council of Churches is engaged in two projects that are somewhat different in kind but both involve forms of ecumenical guidance. The first project is a series of acts that have a good deal of symbolic importance. It involves grants that have been made to resistance movements or movements of liberation in many parts of the world as a sign of the identification of the churches with the victims of racism. The second study is a five-year study, now coming to an end, that opens up new areas for theological and ethical exploration. It is a study on "The Future of Man and Society in a World of Science-based Technology." This has begun a discussion of ethical responsibilities in relation to a baffling complex of problems including those arising from the rapid increase of population and the finiteness of resources. The debate concerns the limits of growth, the threats to the environment, the need for economic justice in the relations between rich and poor nations, and much that goes under the caption "the quality of life." These projects differ from the examples of corporate guidance that I have mentioned so far because the first takes the form of acts more than words, and the second is only the beginning of worldwide thinking about issues that are largely new and answers that are far from clear.

The World Council Assembly at Uppsala in 1968 emphasized the need for the churches to engage in new actions against racism, understood chiefly as white racism. The Central Committee of the World Council, which is a group of about 120 that represents the churches and consists chiefly of their acknowledged leaders, meeting in Canterbury in 1969, made the following decision: "There can be no justice in our world without a transfer of economic resources to undergird the redistribution of political power and to make cultural self-determination meaningful. In this transfer of resources a corporate act of the ecumenical fellowship of churches can provide a significant moral lead."

Those last words were implemented by the decision to grant $200,000 from the World Council's own funds and to seek another $300,000 from its constituency. Grants were to be made to nineteen resistance movements, chiefly in southern Africa, the Portuguese colonies, the Republic of South

Africa, and Rhodesia. Some of these movements were engaged in guerrilla activities and all of them were threats to governments. There was an agreement that the funds would be used for educational and humanitarian programs and not for military purposes. When this action was announced the World Council was furiously attacked in many circles. The South African government commanded the churches in South Africa that were still members of the World Council of Churches to withdraw from it, but they courageously refused to obey while dissociating themselves from this particular action. There was a great deal of debate about the action in West Germany and in Britain, chiefly because movements that were engaged in violence were being supported. In the United States there was less attention given to it, but the *Reader's Digest* was moved to publish two articles that were really diatribes against the World Council, and these articles caused a lot of discussion. While they did stir up feeling against the World Council, they also created a considerable reaction against the *Reader's Digest.*

In spite of the many negative reactions to this unusual political act of the World Council of Churches, the Central Committee, meeting in 1971, unanimously reaffirmed it. As a result, in that year more grants were made, to twenty-four movements—and this time they were on five continents. They included the United Farm Workers in the United States and an Eskimo movement in Canada. Later the Central Committee made additional grants and unanimously decided to extend the fund to $1,000,000.

How is this relevant to our discussion of guidance? The answer is, first, that it was an act that said a great deal to the churches about their responsibility to identify themselves with people oppressed by racism and to do so by supporting political movements that sought to transfer power. Secondly, the process produced more discussion in the churches than any words would have done, and as a result of this discussion minds were changed on a large scale. Churches that had attacked the act at the beginning came around to giving the essential idea their support and to making contributions themselves. This was true of parts of the church in Germany and in Great Britain. I do not know what it means, but gifts were made to this fund by four governments, those of the Netherlands, Sweden, Denmark, and Norway. At least this does indicate that a great many people who could have been expected to be critical were convinced by the Council's act and by its continuous interpretation of it.

One by-product of this action was the appointment of a commission to discuss the theological and ethical issues involved in the use of violence, especially revolutionary violence. After two years of discussion by a widely representative group a report was submitted[10] that usefully analyzed the issues and set forth three different views. One rejected all use of violence. Another sanctioned violence, laying down criteria that must be met if violence is to be justified. The third view (which also sanctioned violence) reflected the experience of those already engaged in revolutionary violence for whom "non-violence does not present itself as an option unless they would withdraw from the struggle for justice." They agreed in rejecting some forms of violence such as "torture in all forms, the holding of innocent hostages and the deliberate or indiscriminate killing of innocent non-combatants." They said of these forms of violence that they "destroy the soul of the perpetrator as surely as the life and health of the victim." While these judgments about limits of violence are, I think, very important, the upshot of this report is that there is nothing new on the basic issue, that the church must recognize more than one view on the question of revolutionary violence as it has done on the question of international war, even though there is growing clarity about the contradiction between most forms of war and Christian faith and ethics.

The World Council's study of "The Future of Man and Society in a World of Science-based Technology" has enlisted a remarkable combination of theologians, social scientists, and physical scientists from all parts of the world. There have been many regional conferences and several conferences that represented the world as a whole, such as the concluding conference, which met in Bucharest in July 1974. This study opened up problems never before faced by churches, such as the relation between recent thinking about the limitation of resources to the problem of justice between nations. In one account of the discussions Roger Shinn reports on the new and still controversial idea about the limits of growth and its impact on the representatives of the developing nations: "To many representatives of the developing countries, the attack on the possibility of continued growth in production came like a thunderclap of doom. One Asian said, 'I am almost tempted to say that, even if it is true, it should not be said' —so devastating did he find the consequences for his own society. Some Latin Americans and Africans wondered whether the whole idea was a plot of the affluent societies to deny to developing countries the gains that their exploiters had already won."[11] There are no conclusions about the particular views advanced by the Club of Rome about the limits of growth, but there is a general acceptance of the finiteness of essential resources. This is related to the rapid growth of population, which is also seen differently in Asia from the way it is seen in the industrialized countries. There is continual debate as to how far social justice would itself lead to the diminution of the rate of the growth of population and concerning the role of government in population control. These issues are obviously related to the vulnerability of the environment and to the means of protecting it. These problems, of which people have become aware only recently, raise profound ethical questions concerning the consumer society in affluent nations. They also raise the question of the religious resources for a movement concerned with the quality of life in a society that makes less use of scarce resources both for its own sake and for the sake of a more just distribution of such resources.

Samuel L. Parmar, an economist from Allahabad Univer-

sity in India and chairman of the Working Group on Church
and Society of the World Council of Churches, which has
supervised this study, has presented assumptions that may
prevail when the idea of the finiteness of resources comes to
be assimilated. He writes as follows:

> The growth process, if patterned on the lines of indus-
> trial nations, causes problems of pollution and of the
> exhaustion of non-renewable resources. That would im-
> ply that our efforts to eradicate poverty will lead to fur-
> ther impoverishment. . . . The solution lies in a radically
> different understanding of economic progress. From a
> resource-destroying mode of production we must move
> to a resource-conserving mode.
> The Asian economic situation is congenial to this out-
> look. Because of limited resources we emphasize auster-
> ity. Of course, under the domination of prevalent ideas
> of growth, austerity is usually recommended as a tempo-
> rary inconvenience in order that material affluence may
> be attained in the near future. Our motive is high-con-
> sumption, our goals quantitative. But the dilemma of
> growth which indicates that the pursuit of quantity will
> lead to further impoverishment should prompt us to
> accept austerity and limitation of wants not simply as
> expediency but as a socially desirable objective. Empha-
> sis on social justice and self-reliance would have similar
> implications.[12]

I have three reasons for reporting briefly on this study.
First, it is a case of pioneering by the churches on a worldwide basis in the attempt to define crucial problems involved
in the future of humanity. Second, the churches are ap-
proaching these questions with no dogmatic answers already
in sight. So far we have little more than questions and raw
material for possible answers. Third, the ecumenical perspective in which this study takes place has led to a relativiz-
ing of the assumptions of the affluent societies, assumptions
that have usually been taken for granted in the churches of

the northern hemisphere. I am sure that, when this material is discussed at the next assembly of the World Council of Churches in 1975, the churches in the northern hemisphere, not least those in the United States, will feel strong pressure from the churches in the Third World to take seriously the way the problems appear to them. This will have been made possible by the missionary movement that established so many of those churches. Today we are learning about unexpected effects of "missions" and about surprises that come from the teaching of the gospel.[13]

IV
The Conflict in American
Churches Over Social Ethics

There is an immense contrast
between all that I have said about the radical imperative and
the actual life and influence of the churches. Evidence that
the radical imperative has had some effect is seen in the
serious conflict today in the churches over the issues of social
justice and the use of national power. The fact of this conflict
is a commonplace of sociological studies of American religion
and also of contemporary journalism. Always, when the conflict is interpreted, the main impact of the churches is seen
to be conservative, and one of their chief interests is seen to
be the avoidance of controversy. The conflict is regarded as
involving in part a difference between the membership of
local churches and denominational, ecumenical, and theological leadership. Also it is regarded in part as a conflict
between the clergy and the laity. In Chapter III examples
were given of some of the issues that have caused conflict in
the recent past. It was a severe trial for the American
churches that they had to deal at the same time with controversies over racial justice and controversies over the American policy in Indochina. As I write, these are not at the center
of attention, and the churches are in a period of relative
quiet. Basic differences in attitude remain and new expressions of conflict may develop at any moment.

Preoccupation with the high-level crimes connected with
Watergate has shifted the emphasis to issues that divide the

country and the churches quite differently from those that I have emphasized. When the facts about Watergate and the many related cases of corruption were unfolded, and as transcripts of the White House tapes were read, traditional standards of personal and public integrity were seen to have been so flagrantly violated that persons at many points on the usual left-right spectrum were equally shocked. Essential issues have been raised by Watergate, but these are not the issues related to social justice and the use of national power which I have most in mind in discussing the implications of the radical imperative.

THE CHURCHES RESIST

There are two basic reasons for the failure of churches to be greatly moved by the radical imperative. The first is the social position of white churches in the northern hemisphere, not least American white churches, which Archbishop Helder Câmara addressed so passionately in the passage I quoted earlier. The second is that aspects of Christian theology as they have been widely understood have given strong support to established institutions or to a privatized form of religion.

I have referred to the dynamism of Christianity as one of the creators of Western civilization. That dynamism caused Christians to be close to the centers of power and privilege in that civilization. This has meant that for them the line of least resistance has been to defend the *status quo*, in which they had a stake and for which they easily found moral and religious justification. As Reinhold Niebuhr said so often, they deceived themselves as much as they deceived others. In a similar vein, sociologists of religion tend to see religion primarily as a support for the ethos of a society, a source of social unity. They tend to play down the function of religion as the source of prophetic criticism.

Max Weber saw in the strong prophetic elements in the

Judeo-Christian tradition the source of the dynamic, future-oriented, innovative, history-making power of that tradition. Are not these very aspects of Christianity responsible for putting Christians into the positions of power and privilege that made them least likely to respond to prophetic criticism of their own institutions? Reinhard Bendix, in his synthetic paraphrase of Weber's thought, says: "The great contribution of the Biblical prophets was to make the morally correct actions of everyday life into a special duty of a people chosen by the mightiest God."[1] In contrast to Weber's analyses of Confucian literati and Brahmin priests, his study entitled *Ancient Judaism* is, as Bendix says, "a study in the sociology of innovation." He goes on to say: "Weber's *Ancient Judaism*, therefore, combines an emphasis upon religious innovators with an analysis of the process by which their unique inspiration became the dominant orientation of the rabbis of post-exilic Judaism, of the Jewish people at large, and, in modified forms, of Western civilization."[2] As one way of explaining the cultural dynamism of our civilization this makes sense. But it seems to me that the contribution of the prophets to the radical criticism of our civilization tends to be submerged.

Weber's better-known analysis of the relation between Protestantism, especially Calvinistic Puritanism, and the rise of capitalism shows in a similar way how aspects of Protestantism were favorable to the virtues needed if capitalistic institutions were to flourish. His emphasis on the need of Calvinists to prove to themselves that they were among the elect by their economic work is so out of line with the Calvinistic emphasis on grace that it is probably overdrawn. Protestantism of many kinds, however, did give a high place to secular callings. It provided a rigorous moral discipline that combined emphasis on the duty to work as a part of the religious life with the "worldly asceticism" that avoided unrestrained consumption and hence made possible the accumulation of capital. This combination certainly provided spiritual support for capitalism, though this was never in the minds of the original Reformers.

Weber makes much of a famous quotation from John Wesley to the effect that "religion must produce both industry and frugality, and these cannot but produce riches." Wesley, troubled about this, says that "the Methodists in every place grow diligent and frugal; consequently they increase in goods. Hence they proportionately increase in pride, in anger, in the desire of the eyes, and the pride of life." He asks: "Is there no way to prevent this—the continual decay of pure religion? We ought not to prevent people from being diligent and frugal; we must exhort all Christians to gain all they can, to save all they can; that is, in effect to grow rich."[3] This quotation brings out Weber's strongest points and it shows that Protestantism, much beyond Calvinistic Puritanism, has favored the ethos of capitalism. So far as Wesley is concerned it should be noted that he also greatly stressed *giving* and that his Methodist movement was a significant factor in the rise of British socialism and in the history of the American social gospel, often in its more radical forms.

The alliance between Protestantism and capitalism produced in the latter part of the nineteenth century a way of thinking that regarded poverty as a sign of sin and wealth as a sign of virtue. Everyone who writes about this chapter in Protestant ethics has a collection of quotations that seem unbelievable when we read them today. Sidney Ahlstrom has chosen two samples that are as shocking as any. Henry Ward Beecher wrote: "No man in this land suffers from poverty unless it be more than his fault—unless it be his *sin.*" That was in the 1870's, and in 1900 William Lawrence, the much-admired Episcopal Bishop of Massachusetts, wrote: "In the long run, it is only to the man of morality that wealth comes."[4] These men were among the most influential churchmen of their time. To read them today is to realize how much the climate has changed within a century.

The residue of this "Protestant ethic," which is generally opposed today by Protestant theologians and by the corpo-

rate thinking of most Protestant churches, remains a powerful factor in the social conservatism of the American Protestant community. Martin Marty, in his *Righteous Empire*,
which gives great emphasis to this side of the American Protestant heritage, quotes the historian of American culture,
Henry F. May, as saying: "In 1876 Protestantism presented
a massive, almost unbroken front in the defense of the social
status quo." Marty adds: "Later historians may be tempted
to be revisionist about their predecessors' judgments on the
American past but is difficult to find documentation that
would lead one to alter May's judgment."[5] Today as one
reads the results of questionnaires used by sociologists of
religion one may well think that the defense of the social
status quo is still massive. But it is far from being unbroken,
and hence there is conflict in the churches over social ethics.

The second explanation of the contrast between the radical imperative and the life of the churches is the continuing
influence of certain theological ideas that I mentioned in
Chapter I. The combination of otherworldly individualism
with conservative interpretations of divine providence have
given religious sanction to the dominant social institutions
and rationalizations for resistance to radical social change.
The fact that the New Testament writers never had to face
any political responsibility has made it possible to read the
New Testament, even the Gospels, in terms of a privatistic
interpretation of Christianity. Paternalistic forms of love,
which have often been sincere, have generally been sufficient to satisfy the Christian conscience in spite of the injustice of social structures, the maldistribution of wealth, and
the actual human condition. Nationalistic expressions of
Christianity have added to the moral confusion. Reinhold
Niebuhr's discernment of the paradox in patriotism, i.e., that
"patriotism transmutes individual unselfishness into national
egoism,"[6] suggests part of the dynamism behind this confusion. Also, there is the providential sanction for particular
governments as well as for nationality itself, and there is an

arsenal of false idealisms that facilitate the identification of God with the nation's cause. Capitalism, imperialism, and militarism have had such strong Christian support that it is no wonder churches have lost a great deal of moral credibility. In the recent past the fact that adversaries in the cold war, and in the hot war in Indochina, were avowedly atheistic has provided additional religious support for national policies that are now widely rejected on religious and moral grounds. This is part of the conflict.

Many of the sociological studies of this conflict emphasize the difference between the clergy and the laity. This is true, for example, of Jeffrey K. Hadden's *The Gathering Storm in the Churches*, published in 1969.[7] Its subtitle is: A Sociologist's View of the Widening Gap Between Clergy and Laymen." The statistics with which this book is full are appalling. Here is one typical example. The following statement was presented to samples of white clergy and laity. The respondents were asked to say whether they agreed with it or not: "Negroes would be better off if they would take advantage of the opportunities that have been made available to them rather than spending so much time protesting." Of the laity, 86 percent agreed. Only 35 percent of the clergy agreed. That may seem to be too many clergy on the side of complacency, but the contrast between the two groups is quite remarkable. It is also worth noting that when the figures were broken down by religious communities, 89 percent of Protestants and 84 percent of Catholics agreed while only 65 percent of Jews agreed. This finding is interesting because it indicates that Jews, even when they are economically privileged, understand what it means to be in a minority. This is significant today in view of the unfortunate tension between Jews and blacks over quotas and other issues.[8]

A study by Rodney Stark and others entitled *Wayward Shepherds*[9] showed that, of the Protestant clergy of California—studied across the board in both conservative and liberal denominations—more than a third were silent in the pulpit on the Indochina war and on a vote in California on a proposition calling for the repeal of an open housing law in 1964, which was a kind of test case that deeply divided the churches. These writers are impressed by the silence of so many of the clergy on social issues. They have a great deal of evidence to show a close correlation between conservative theological and conservative social attitudes. Since they stress many of the same theological convictions that I have mentioned, we have here confirmation of the effect of theology. These authors say that "it is because of their religious convictions that many Protestant clergymen reject the relevance of speaking out from the pulpit or elsewhere on social issues."[10] I am more impressed than they are by the fact that two thirds of the clergy did regard it as their responsibility to preach on these social issues. Notice that the example from Hadden's study also shows that approximately one third of the white clergy were complacent about the oppression of black people.

Dean M. Kelley, of the staff of the National Council of Churches, has provided considerable evidence in his book, *Why Conservative Churches Are Growing*,[11] that those churches which are conservative theologically and socially and are exclusive in their teaching are growing at the expense of those which have the more progressive outlook. He has said that he had originally chosen as the title for his book "Why Strict Churches Are Strong." In the main-line, progressive denominations there is a downward curve in numerical strength, a sharp decline in financial resources available beyond the local congregation, and a serious slump in morale. To some extent this is a result of the conflict over social issues, which has been at times ugliest in such denominations. Kelley believes that the progressive churches have not offered people a gospel that gives meaning for their lives. I am sure that there is considerable truth in this. Both in the period of the flowering of liberalism and in the period of the strength of neo-orthodoxy there was a more confident message than now. The impression that one gets from studies of contemporary American Christianity is that those who emphasize the radical imperative are weak compared with the conservative opposition and that this opposition is supported by a resurgence of an uncritically orthodox theology.

In what follows I shall first describe several countervailing factors that give a somewhat different picture of the present situation. I shall then deal with what I believe to be the deepest issue in the current conflict. It is a problem that stems from the two competing roles of the church as pastoral sustainer and as prophetic disturber, from the need to do justice both to the radical imperative and to the mediation of grace.

COUNTERVAILING FACTORS

The first countervailing factor is a global view of the theological and social differences among Christians. When this becomes real, ideas of the meaning of conservatism and liberalism are seen to need some revising. Conservative theologies in many other countries are not as much tied to conservative or even rightist politics as is often the case in this country. Right-wing Americanism naturally has no appeal outside our borders, and it is precisely this type of religious expression in the United States that is responsible for a great deal of the heat in the present conflict in the churches. Consider, for example, the Bangkok conference called by the World Council of Churches on "Salvation Today." Because of its connection with the World Council, many Americans whose "evangelicalism" is tied to a rejection of "ecumenism" dismiss the Bangkok conference as a manifestation of "liberalism." I think, however, that on any fair reading of the materials from the conference it would be seen to transcend the stereotypes of theology that divide the American churches. The use of the word "evangelical" by one group within American Protestantism is confusing because in Europe the word is used widely as an equivalent of "Protestant." However, this is an American usage that one can hardly avoid in the context of this chapter. "Evangelical" refers to a broad movement the dynamism of which is not suggested by "conservative," and which is not fairly identified with "fundamentalism." I want to emphasize the point that an ecumenical perspective does not generally lead to preoccupation with an ingrown, if worldwide, *Christian* community. The bishops of Chile have given the whole church a very helpful phrase to describe their true role. In appealing for the rights of those who are persecuted by the post-Allende government of Chile they said: "The Church must be the voice of all, especially of those who have no voice."

The second countervailing factor is that those who project the demise of open and intellectually self-critical forms of Christianity (I try here to avoid the designation "liberal") do so in the face of a long-term trend to the contrary. American church history has been the movement of denominations from uncritical orthodoxy and exclusivism toward a more critical theology (not necessarily to be identified with anyone's stereotype of "liberalism") and toward a more open attitude to other churches. The recent retrogression in the Lutheran Church—Missouri Synod is the kind of exception that proves the rule. While under pressure from a reactionary denominational president the ecclesiastical body has moved backward. But the vast majority of the faculty of the Missouri Synod's Concordia Seminary in St. Louis have resisted this trend courageously. They have risked their careers by establishing a free seminary not sanctioned by the denomination rather than conform to the dictates of the present ecclesiastical authorities. It is true of theological schools quite generally that when theological scholarship is taken seriously the movement of thought within them is away from uncritical orthodoxy and exclusivism. The influence of international scholarship is extremely important in changing enclaves of scholarly provincialism. It would be invidious for me to name institutions at this point, but Concordia Seminary itself is an illustration of this trend. Also many observers have recently called attention to the way Fuller Theological Seminary, which flourishes as a part of the growing strength of conservative evangelicalism, has in recent years moved from right to center. There is great concern among its faculty and students for social justice and peace.

I doubt if the ecumenical significance of the cooperation of theological schools has ever been sufficiently recognized. The American Association of Theological Schools was established to improve the standards of theological education and to provide many services to the schools without representing any theological preferences as such. Through its system of accreditation and through its provision of fellowships for sabbatical study for seminary professors it has done a great deal to raise standards of scholarship and teaching. In many other ways it has been an instrument for cooperation between schools. It has no theological ax to grind, but its influence inevitably breaks down exclusivisms and the dogmas that support them. It has done much to encourage the trend toward clusters of theological schools that include both Protestant and Catholic institutions and inevitably expose uncritical orthodoxies to criticism. The influence of Catholics in these clusters is extremely important. They have the effect of a kind of third force because their commitment to tradition is so often combined with openness to contemporary thought and to radical social concerns. In my experience, both in New York City and in Berkeley, California, I have noted how effectively Jesuits challenge both uncritical orthodoxies and social conservatism. In protest against these trends new and more protected theological schools are formed, just as new and more protected denominations have been formed so often in the past. But they too are likely to change in the course of one or two generations. I am not arguing for any particular theological conclusions, but I think that it is very difficult to protect theologies or churches against self-criticism and what I call "openness" for long.

The third countervailing factor I see is the experience of the church by Protestants as including in a living way the Roman Catholic Church. So long as I assumed that my church, the church to which I looked for inspiration and guidance, was limited to worldwide Protestantism, my church was sadly truncated. This was actually true of me until the late 1950's, and I doubt if I was exceptionally bigoted in such matters.

Today ethical inspirations and stimuli come as much from the Roman Catholic community as from the Protestant community so far as my experience is concerned. Often I think that they come even more from the worldwide Catholic community. American Catholicism has not only been profoundly changed in its ecumenical relations and in its theological orientation by the Second Vatican Council, but it has also been transformed by the erosion of absolutistic and strident anti-Communism in the whole church from the Vatican down. There has also been the passing of the superpatriotism of early generations of American Catholics who, as recent Americans, sought to prove their Americanism. The present generation of Catholics, especially after the election to the presidency of John F. Kennedy, feels no need to do this. There have been no more radical criticisms of American policy in Indochina than those that have come from the Catholic community. I am not thinking only of the more dramatic protests of the Berrigans but of innumerable voices among priests and nuns and lay persons that have been heard among the dissenters. The lay Catholic journal *Commonweal* has been one of the most forthright of all religious journals in its opposition to the Government's war policy. In November 1971, somewhat belatedly, the Roman Catholic bishops came out against the war, labeling it in classical terms an "unjust war."

Pope Paul VI, in his encyclical *Populorum Progressio,*
provided a basis for liberation movements within the church
(i.e., of Catholics in Latin America and elsewhere) that struggle for radical change. There is good reason to expect that the
radical Catholicism which has arisen in Latin America will
influence Catholics in this country and that they will become
a much stronger force than American Protestants in working
for changes in our Government's stance in relation to Latin
America. It is at least a beginning that the American Catholic
bishops have strongly criticized the governments of Brazil
and of post-Allende Chile for their violations of human rights.
They asked the United States Government to bring pressure
on Brazil and went so far as to ask our Government "to
condition its financial aid and military assistance to Chile
upon the demonstration that human and civil rights have
been restored in the country." This is remarkable because
Brazil is a capitalistic country, a favorite of the American
Government and of American business. The junta's action in
overthrowing the Allende regime in Chile brought great
satisfaction in Washington and in board rooms throughout
the country. There is the shocking revelation in testimony to
a Congressional committee by William E. Colby, the head of
the Central Intelligence Agency, that the C.I.A. had fun-
neled more than $8,000,000 into Chile to prevent the elec-
tion of President Allende and then to undermine his
regime.[12] This is an appalling example of policies of the Government of the United States in relation to Latin America
that may well create a major conflict between our Government and churches with the Catholic Church taking the lead.

On June 5, 1974, there was a crowded service in the cathe-
dral in Santiago, Chile, in honor of Raúl Cardinal Silva Hen-
ríquez. The cardinal had done what he could to cooperate
with the Allende regime after it had come to power. After
the military counterrevolution that overthrew the Allende
regime, he addressed himself to the protection of dissenters
and to reconciliation in the country. In its report of the ser-

vice, *The New York Times* said: "The audience today, mostly poor and lower-middle-class people, included relatives of political prisoners and many sympathizers of the Allende government who have come to look on the Cardinal and an important segment of the Catholic Church as their protectors.... With the dissolution of Congress, political parties and labor unions, the church has gradually become the main vehicle of dissent for critics of the junta's harsh measures."[13]

In times of crisis there can be a great advantage in having a highly visible hierarchy. Cardinal Silva had the support of the Chilean hierarchy, which spoke out strongly against the junta's use of torture, of arbitrary and lengthy detentions, and of an economic policy that increased the burdens of the poor. The hierarchy has played the same role of defender of human rights in other Latin-American countries—Brazil, Paraguay, Bolivia, and Guatemala, to name a few examples. In the Philippines also, Catholics, with some support from the hierarchy, have been struggling at great risk against the tyranny of President Ferdinand Marcos. In South Korea, where Protestantism is much stronger, Catholics and Protestants have joined in a similar struggle. As has been the case so often in the past, courage is given to the church when it is up against the wall. Today it defends not only itself and its own members but also the rights of all people who are victims of cruel and arbitrary political power. This seems to be a period of low expectation for the church in the United States. We can be helped in our own morale to observe today that elsewhere under great difficulties the church has risen to the occasion.

There is a long-standing commitment on the part of Catholic leaders in this country to social justice in the United States. Their involvement in the labor movement goes back to the late nineteenth century; it grew as the struggle to organize the industrial workers into unions became intense. Today the remarkable commitment of both the hierarchy and the religious orders to the cause of the United Farm Workers union

shows that this concern for economic justice is still important. Roman Catholicism, unlike Protestantism, has always
kept some distance from capitalism. It has opposed socialism
because of its traditional support of limited rights of private
property and because of its antipathy toward Marxism on
theological grounds. But in recent years doctrinaire opposition to all forms of socialism has been abandoned and the
antipathy to Marxism has greatly diminished. Indeed, Catholics and Marxists often cooperate, especially in Latin America.

It may be said that the Catholic Church as an institution
has suffered from the progressive influence that stems from
Vatican II and especially from the theological emancipation
that has developed since Pope John opened the windows.
The church is deeply divided and people no longer go to
mass out of fear. Attendance at mass in the United States in
1973 dropped by 13 percent. Many priests have left the
priesthood and the number of new vocations has been so
reduced that there is a real threat to the future of the church
as regards leadership. For many Catholics there are debilitat-
ing confusion and something close to a loss of religious identity. These are the natural consequences of drastic changes,
especially of the movement away from authoritarianism and
exclusivism. Yet the Roman Catholic community that
emerges from this turmoil may well claim a more spontane-
ous loyalty and Christian experience may be more deeply
personal. The astounding growth of charismatic Catholicism
is one sign of this. Statistical loss will still leave an enormous
Catholic community, and it may well be a more vital one,
from which non-Catholics can receive guidance and inspiration for their social ethics.

The fourth countervailing factor that may alter the present
pattern of polarization is the emergence of a new generation
of conservative evangelicals who, holding to their theological
and evangelistic concerns, are committed to a radical understanding of Christian social responsibility. The evidence for

this new development has begun to accumulate rapidly. Considerable attention has been given in the religious press to the conference of evangelical leaders in Chicago in November 1973, which emphasized evangelical need for a new social stance. About fifty persons signed the "Declaration of Evangelical Social Concern" that came out of the conference, and among these were many national leaders of the movement. That declaration is a complete repudiation of the close link between "evangelicalism" and uncritical Americanism. The following sentences give some idea of the spirit and the trend of thought contained in the declaration:

> We acknowledge that God requires justice. But we have not proclaimed or demonstrated his justice to an unjust American society. Although the Lord calls us to defend the social and economic rights of the poor and the oppressed, we have mostly remained silent. We deplore the historic involvement of the church in America with racism and the conspicuous responsibility of the evangelical community for perpetuating the personal attitudes and institutional structures that have divided the body of Christ along color lines. Further, we have failed to condemn the exploitation of racism at home and abroad by our economic system. . . . We acknowledge our Christian responsibilities of citizenship. Therefore, we must challenge the misplaced trust of the nation in economic and military might—a proud trust that promotes a national pathology of war and violence which victimizes our neighbors at home and abroad. We must resist the temptation to make the nation and its institutions objects of near-religious loyalty.

There is much more, but this is enough to suggest that new voices are coming from this important segment of Protestantism.

Richard Quebedeaux's book, *The Young Evangelicals*,[14] provides a great deal of documentation concerning these new trends of thought and commitment. Many members of

the new generation reject completely the tendency to identify the Bible with capitalism, with the American way of life,
with American policy abroad, with anti-Communism as the
rationalization for the support of political rightism. A new
journal that came rather spontaneously from this group is
entitled *Post-American* to express this repudiation of so
much of the social emphases in the evangelical past. The
leading editorial in the issue for June and July 1974 says:
"Young evangelicals regard the U.S. role in Indo-China as a
moral obscenity matched only by the official (evangelical)
silence and support for American war policy."

I first became aware that this change was taking place
when I learned that the triennial missionary convention in
1970 of the Inter-Varsity student movement—a gathering of
10,000 students in Urbana, Illinois—refused to invite Billy
Graham to speak to the convention, though in the past he
had always been invited. Quebedeaux says that this refusal to
invite Graham was repeated in 1973.

Many pervasive influences have entered into this development. There are ways of reading the Bible that free it from
imposed patterns of interpretation (e.g., the pattern of "dis-
pensationalism"). There is a greater emphasis on the prophets as interpreters of the social issues of their own times (i.e.,
not as mouthpieces of abstract "prophecy"), and more emphasis on the teachings of Jesus. I have noted the influence
of two quite specific groups: first, blacks who are "evangelical" Protestants, who share the outrage of other blacks
against the racism of the white churches, and who are fully
committed to the black cause (a cause that requires radical
social change); and second, representatives of some Mennonite denominations and of the Church of the Brethren,
churches that combine a strong evangelical tradition with
absolute pacifism and that are completely alien to uncritical
Americanism.

I believe that Billy Graham—in spite of many things in his
record that are on the plus side, such as his cooperative

ecumenical spirit and his early attitude toward civil rights, expressed in his refusal to speak to segregated audiences—has done a great disservice to the American churches. He has allowed himself to be used by American presidents to give religious sanction to their policies. His claim to be neutral about the issue of the Indochina war was absurd, because in his position silence was interpreted as giving consent to the national policy. He caused confusion by suggesting that the war was only a political issue. He was shocked by the Watergate tapes and he conveyed the idea that swearing and lying are breaches of morality but that bombing helpless people relentlessly for years is only a matter of politics. His saying that he was a New Testament evangelist and not an Old Testament prophet separates two roles that should not be separated. If he leaves out of the evangelistic message all that might be learned from the prophets, he misleads the converted about the meaning of their conversion.

It is encouraging to me that many of the young evangelicals are dissatisfied with Billy Graham on these scores. Two of his basic convictions seem to be responsible for the weakness of his social message. His frequent use of a literal interpretation of the idea of the second coming of Christ gives assurance that social evils can be expected to increase before that event and that Christ in his coming will set things right. Then there is his assumption that if people are once converted to an individualistic gospel, they will as individuals change society. This fails to account for the fact that converted Christians so generally share the prejudices and the blind spots of their social groups. Quebedeaux does not exaggerate when he as an evangelical says in criticism of Graham: "Saved individuals are often (probably most often) supporters of the *status quo* rather than social change."[15]

We can see in this development evidence of a modification of the monolithic social conservatism of the growing evangelical community. This should remove some of the emotion from the church conflict over social ethics. It will be a wel-

come change to have many witnesses among Protestant theological conservatives to the Biblical basis for the radical
social imperative. Conflicts in the church will continue, but
they will be much more healthy when "ecumenist" Protestants and Roman Catholics and conservative evangelicals
unite in commitment to many social goals.

Amen.

Priest + Prophet

GRACE AND LAW

There is a deeper source of conflict in the churches. We see
it on two levels. The more superficial level is the conflict
between those for whom the church is an agent of social
change and those for whom it is a haven from the disturb-
ances of the world. The deeper level involves the contrast
between prophetic ethics and grace, often identified, especially by Lutherans, as a contrast between law and gospel. To
separate these two levels in detail is artificial, yet I believe
that it is important to distinguish between a partly secula-
rized search for support and comfort, and a strongly Christian emphasis on grace and forgiveness. How varied are the
pastoral needs of the same person, and of the same family, at
different times. The distinction between the two levels that
I make here should not be directed against any person who
turns to the church when life is especially difficult, or against
the church that ministers to such need. But if we think of a
wide spectrum of ministries and forms of religious expression, some would be nearer the "comfort" end of the spectrum than others.

I take the word "comfort" from the book entitled *To Comfort and to Challenge,*[16] a study of The Episcopal Church in
the United States. Its findings reflect the experience of many
other denominations as indicated by other studies. The authors found that the dominant role of the church in the
minds of most members is associated with the word "comfort," while a minority see their religion as one of prophetic
challenge. One of the findings in the study is that a large

proportion of church members are psychologically deprived and find in their religion and in their participation in the life of the church a compensation for relative failure or for a sense of inferiority. Loneliness is often the greatest deprivation, and the church provides community. Women and older persons often are in this situation of deprivation, and they make up a large part of the active membership of churches. The authors are highly doubtful that churches with their present constituencies can be at the same time both agents of comfort and agents of challenge, though they suggest that there can be units within churches that emphasize challenge.

Concern for comfort goes with the avoidance of controversy and there are many persons in the leadership of churches who want above all things to prevent initiatives that may commit their church to any position in a controversy. This is a continual problem in the relation between a local church and the larger units of the denomination or larger body to which it belongs. The larger units often make statements or authorize actions that are resented by the members of local churches because they regard themselves as misrepresented. While such positions (whether taken by the regional judicatory, the national assembly, or beyond that the ecumenical councils) are often interpreted technically as speaking *to* rather than *for* the local churches, this is usually not understood either by members or by the press. When ministers preach on controversial issues, they speak *to* the congregation rather than for the congregation. Yet the visibility of the ministers as representatives of their churches to the outside world means that their message not only disturbs the calm of the hour of worship but also causes anxiety among the worshipers, because some of them fear that what is said will be understood outside the church as representing them.

The word "comfort" brings out the contrast that the authors of the study want to stress, but taken by itself it trivializes the Christian experience. This is not true when comfort is a by-product of faith and trust, of a sense that one's life has meaning in the presence of God. There is nothing trivial about the comfort that reflects the faith that "if we live, we live to the Lord, and if we die, we die to the Lord; so then, whether we live or whether we die, we are the Lord's" (Rom. 14:8). The liturgies of the churches express the unity of comfort and challenge, for they combine confession and repentance with the assurance of forgiveness. They combine the tragic realism of the cross with the divine victory and the human hope expressed in the resurrection faith. This unity of true comfort and judgment is often lost in actual experience even though the words are regularly used. The concrete realities of sin and disobedience are covered over by generalizations that have lost their edge. Then the generalized confession is so swallowed up by the assurance of forgiveness that even the realization that the destructive consequences of sin continue in the lives of others becomes dim or disappears. This orthodox form of what Dietrich Bonhoeffer called "cheap grace" is paralleled by an optimistic and progressivistic liberalism that H. Richard Niebuhr described in his famous passage about those who taught "that a God without wrath brought men without sin into a kingdom without judgment through the ministrations of a Christ without a cross."[17] This is perhaps a verbal cartoon, but it has the truth often found in cartoons.

The deeper contrast is between the radical imperative and the gospel of forgiveness. The radical imperative is a dynamic form of law that demands more than our codified moralisms or legalisms. If this were the only Christian teaching, then the more sensitive a person was, the more surely it would be a road to despair. On the other hand the gospel of forgiveness can be so preached and taught that it blots out continuing concern about the social consequences of sin. There is a long-standing debate as to whether the law with its judgment should be preached first, in order to prepare people to receive the gospel, or whether the gospel should be preached first, enabling people to receive truth calling for repentance without having to defend themselves against it. I think that within the church exposure to both law and gospel at almost the same time is possible and that the exact nuances that are best in any particular case of preaching or teaching should be left to the situation. Forgiveness does free people to face the realities of their own lives with full honesty. Also, it frees them for a forgiving attitude toward others. Charity and mercy toward those whose sins are less respectable than one's own or toward those who are on the other side of a conflict from oneself are in short supply, and without them there is no hope of overcoming the self-righteous intransigence that tears apart so much of the world. A one-sided emphasis upon forgiveness and justification to the neglect of what is technically and pretentiously called "sanctification" is often charged against those, such as Reinhold Niebuhr, who put their chief stress on justification. But this charge is based on a failure to realize that the fruits of justification should be honesty about oneself, mercy toward others, and gratitude to God. These are themselves a large part of the content of "sanctification" or of growth in Christian character.

The social effect, often unintended, of this aspect of Christian experience is well described by British historian Herbert Butterfield in his book *Christianity and History*. He says that in one fundamental sense "Christianity alone attacks the seat of evil in the kind of world we have been considering, and has a solvent for the intellectual predicaments that arise in such a world. It addresses itself precisely to that crust of self-righteousness which, by the nature of its teaching, it has to dissolve before it can do anything else with a man.... And though conflict might still be inevitable in history even if this particular evil did not exist, there can be no doubt that its presence multiplies the deadlocks and gravely deepens all the tragedies of all the centuries."[18]

There is always a great deal of tension between law and

gospel. I had an interesting experience of this tension at a
national student conference many years ago. Lesslie Newbigin, the brilliant bishop of the Church of South India and
moving leader of thought about the mission of the church,
gave a series of devotional addresses. One morning he spoke
about Paul's attitude toward the law and its limitations in
relation to Christian salvation. He did a thorough job of this,
and the law seemed to be disposed of for the moment. He
was immediately followed by Martin Luther King, Jr., who
was at the height of his struggle for racial justice. King made
it quite clear that his cause greatly needed both the moral
law and changes in the law of the state. The contrast between
these two presentations was striking, and the audience was
very much aware of it, and a day or so later Bishop Newbigin
in another address brought the issue of the law back again.
That episode does not mean that either speaker was wrong
in what he said, but the contrast reflected a deep tension
especially in Protestant theology.

If one uses the words "comfort" and "challenge" with the
deeper level of this contrast in mind, one of the experiences
that upsets any simplistic view of the contrast is the discovery
that sooner or later the challengers need comfort. For a short
period enthusiasm for a cause may keep them going. The
sense that one is responding to the claims of truth and justice
or to the dictates of compassion may be enough for morale.
Commitments of this kind can unify one's life for a time. But
complexities overtake these simplified commitments. Even
successes create new and unanticipated problems and actual
alternatives call for new and troublesome decisions. Those
whose lives have been unified by devotion to a particular
cause that has the right to claim their allegiance often find
that such changes make it necessary to find some new mark
of identity.

I can remember a period in which the right of labor to
organize unions independent of management was believed
to be the one essential key to a future of greater social justice.

While labor organizations are still extremely important in representing a large part of the population whose interests would be neglected or overridden without them, they have often become static institutions with limited objectives and with little concern for those outside their membership, especially racial minorities. Also the experience of labor leaders who in the 1930's had to struggle against Communist factions in their unions and who were deeply influenced by the anti-Communism of the cold war often made them opponents of reconciliation with Communist countries in the 1960's and 1970's, and hawkish in their support of the war in Indochina. Another example is the frustration that has been caused by splits in the black community that occurred just after the movement for civil rights was at its peak. This is a problem for committed blacks, and it complicates the role of whites with similar commitments.

Prophetic challenge may produce a paralyzing sense of guilt, but acting primarily out of such guilt may distort the person who acts and the cause that is served. How can a sense of hopeless guilt be transformed into a future-oriented sense of responsibility? Guilt has a place, but grace that so transforms it may deliver persons and their movements for change from rigidity, from intermittent despair, and from a compensating destructive self-righteousness.

I believe that theological discussion of these issues has emphasized sin and guilt too exclusively and has not paid enough attention to human finiteness. Today we need courage to persevere in spite of sin and its consequences and also in spite of the sheer scale and complexity of our problems. So many of them are global problems, and there is a degree of unmanageability about them that is not chiefly the result of sin. If on a global scale neighbors were truly open to each other's needs without being held back by the sinful exaggeration of preference on all sides for one's own community, with only minimal concessions to the needs of other communities, some obstacles to the solution of the problems of world hunger would be overcome. But worldwide planning of production and distribution of food would still involve great difficulties. If a world political structure with power to direct production and distribution were necessary, not only would it be subject to the sins of corrupt dealing and of ethnocentric foot-dragging, but it would also be subject to the difficulty of planning and of implementing plans on such a vast scale. There would probably be coercion, and this would be a consequence of sin; but it would also be a consequence of the difficulty of securing the essential synchronizing and meshing of an enormous variety of activities, which has roots also in our finiteness. When one speaks of coercion on such a scale, think of the threats to freedom, to the values in widespread decentralization of human initiatives, as well as to the values in freedom to dissent. Here is a complex of problems that are doubtless greatly intensified by sin but that also come from the tension between competing values as these values are honestly weighed differently by different people, by different communities. There is also the age-old difficulty of inventing institutions that will do justice to these competing values.

Forgiveness for recognized and confessed sin is fundamental, but also I believe that there is need for healing and fresh morale and courage in the face of frustrations and miseries of this other sort. The challengers and the challenged need gospel and support as well as challenge. The radical imperative is not enough. Those who respond to that imperative in their own place and time need to be grasped by the reality of God's presence regardless of which way the tides of history flow. They need to be inspired and sustained by the vision of God's ultimate rule without allowing that vision to undercut a sense of the urgency of battling against particular wrongs and achieving limited goals. They need to see life under the signs of both cross and resurrection. The struggle for social goals soon becomes a deeply personal pilgrimage.

V
Theologies of Liberation

There is a converging of a great many contemporary theologians and schools of theology, both Protestant and Roman Catholic, on common themes that are central for a radical Christian social ethic. Consider some of the labels that theologians have adopted: "political theology," "theology of hope," "theology of revolution," "liberation theology," "black theology." Some of the main themes are as follows: that God is with new emphasis the God of the future, that for humanity the future is open, with Christian eschatological hope lifting the hope of humanity's future in history, that the world is where the church ministers, that there is need for political action to change the structures of society with varying attitudes to illegal or violent revolutionary strategies, that theology and piety have been distorted by individualism and privatism, that once again the promise of the Kingdom of God is central for the Christian hope and for the direction of Christian ethics. I am far from suggesting that these various theological initiatives or schools of thought can be harmonized, but all commit the church and the Christian to social and political change. All are moved in different ways by the radical imperative.

There is a wide spectrum on issues of revolution. On the one hand there is Wolfhart Pannenberg, who stresses the centrality of the Kingdom of God and is hopeful about the future, but who opposes radical changes that threaten the gains of past revolutions built into present European structures. On the other hand there is Gustavo Gutiérrez, who writes in a revolutionary or prerevolutionary Latin-American situation. His theology of liberation takes for granted the moral necessity of a revolutionary overturning of oppressive powers and structures. Both Pannenberg and Gutiérrez stress the Kingdom of God as the goal of history. Perhaps somewhere between them is Jürgen Moltmann with his "theology of hope," which is more open to revolutionary change of structures and which is based on a real concern about situations in the Third World that call for a radical break with the past. Moltmann, however, more than Gutiérrez, emphasizes the temptations of the revolutionaries and the dangers to freedom that come after a revolution. It says a good deal that Moltmann is greatly indebted for his emphasis on the future to the free Marxist philosopher Ernst Bloch. Black theologians such as James Cone write out of the experience of being oppressed as black people in the United States and uniquely concentrate on white racism as the chief enemy of justice and humanity. There is an extraordinary ferment among women, who have come to a new awareness of the subordinate role, the second-class human condition, to which they have been consigned by male-dominated culture and, not least, by male-dominated churches and theology. There is in the making a theology of women's liberation that consists in a massive theological attack on the sexist presuppositions and language of traditional theology and of the polity and liturgy of churches together with a new and constructive expression.

Besides mentioning theologies that are recent in origin I should add comments on the heritage of both Karl Barth and Dietrich Bonhoeffer, and on the very different "process theology," which is emphasized chiefly in the United States. First, regarding Karl Barth: His emphasis on redemption rather than creation was favorable to an emphasis on the radically new in history. His political outlook always reflected his early socialism and his intense anticapitalism. In the conflict between the socialist-Communist East and the capitalist West, Barth generally gave the benefit of the doubt to the former. Dietrich Bonhoeffer was not a social revolutionary but he believed that Christ was a present reality within political life. Bonhoeffer found himself facing some of the same kinds of decisions involving illegal action and the use of violence that are part of the life of social revolutionaries in many situations. He too stressed the positive significance of the world and of the new. Finally, process theology provides a metaphysical framework for a dynamic, future-oriented conception of God and it emphasizes the positive significance of the world and the centrality of human community.

The themes that I have stressed have dominated ecumenical social theology for decades. All corporate Christian thinking under the ecumenical umbrella has taken with utmost seriousness both the human effects of long-term technological revolutions and the aspirations and dilemmas of those who are now engaged in social revolution or those who see the need for such engagement. Across the whole world the question of the justification of revolutionary violence deeply divides Christians. I have an impression that it divides observers more than it does those who live in revolutionary or prerevolutionary situations.

The Christian response to official Communism and to Marxism as a social diagnosis or as a general approach to social change is more positive now than when the cold war determined attitudes. Today it is generally understood that there is no one monolithic Communism and there is very little of the absolutistic religious anti-Communism that was so influential as recently as a decade ago. The Christian-Marxist dialogue may be less active now than it was when a humanistic Marxism was flourishing in Czechoslovakia. The center of Christian-Marxist relations (consisting more of cooperation in concrete situations than dialogue on abstractions) has moved

from Europe to Latin America. There has been a positive
response to the achievements of Chinese Communism and
an awareness that Maoism has made a principle of a continuing dialectic or of permanent revolution—in sharp contrast
to Communism as influenced chiefly by Leninism and Stalinism. These are most significant developments. One standard theological criticism of Communism has always been
that it assumed that a permanent utopia would someday
follow the revolution and that the dialectic would then come
to a fulfillment and an end. I remember the astonishment
that came over me when I read that a missionary bulletin of
the Vatican had hailed the Christian elements in the
thoughts of Chairman Mao.

I believe that the Marxist rejection of all religion and the
dogmatic atheism of Communist parties and governments
are profoundly tragic. They are a judgment upon the
churches for their inconsistent combination of privatism in
religion and alliance with oppressive powers. But that does
not alter the tragic consequences of the official closing of
doors to Christian influences both in educational systems and
in all the media of communication. There is some loosening
up of this antireligious stance among Communists in Western
Europe, and there are variations in the countries of Eastern
Europe, in some of which the churches have considerable
strength. The pressure of official antireligious policies, however, continues. Sometimes the churches gain inner strength
from this very pressure, and even in the Soviet Union it is
remarkable that between thirty and fifty million people are
still active believers aboveground. Below the surface there is
widespread skepticism about or indifference toward atheism.
And there is considerable underground Christian expression
that is hostile to the accommodations the church has made.

THE LIBERATION OF WOMEN

I shall deal first with the liberation of women. This is closer
to more readers, whether they are men or women, than any

other form of liberation. Also, I must confess that its importance has been for me quite a recent discovery. Rosemary
Ruether says: "The oppression of women is undoubtedly the
oldest form of oppression in human history."[1] If I had read
that statement five years ago, I would have doubted its validity. I would have thought the word "oppression" an over-
statement for a phenomenon considered so universal. I was
too much impressed by the privileges enjoyed by middle-
class and upper-class women, and by the informal and indirect forms of power often exercised by them, and by the
fact that so many women seemed satisfied with their condition. Today I am more impressed both by the extraordinary
burden of an imposed status of inferiority and subjection
from which women have suffered through the ages and by
the injustices and the indignities from which they still suffer
even after they have won many rights and opportunities
formerly denied them. Also, I never get over amazement at
the extent to which the Christian tradition (including such
great teachers as Augustine and Thomas Aquinas) has been
responsible for the idea that women have an essential inferiority to men in nature and that they do not reflect the divine
image in the full sense in which men do. It took a long time
for this idea to die, but its effects are still with us.

Women have been treated as ritually impure, as the property of their husbands or at least, according to most theologians until now, called by God to be subject to their husbands. They have (in a special way, exemplified by Eve) been
regarded as the sources of sin, the temptresses of men. This
view is often held with great concern by celibates. Women
have been believed to be intellectually inferior to men, to
belong to the bodily and irrational side of human experience
rather than to the world of mind and spirit. Until quite recently their right to education was controversial and access
to higher education was denied to them. They had to struggle for the right to vote even in the most advanced democ-
racies including our own country well into this century. The
propaganda against women's suffrage showed how deep was

the assumption of their inferiority and their subordinate role in our culture. Though women have had the vote in this country since 1920, they are only now beginning to hold positions of political power. They are exploited by the media as mindless sex objects; they are accustomed to hear themselves spoken of as "the opposite sex" and to find themselves set apart with poor jokes at their expense. They have been and are victims of severe discrimination insofar as advancement is concerned when they work in business or the professions. When women have jobs—and today they constitute about 40 percent of the American labor force—they are paid much less than men for the same work, even though a great many of them are the chief support of their families. In the churches, even when ordination is open to them, women seldom have opportunities to serve that fit their gifts and their training. Churches that still refuse them ordination keep alive the ancient myths and prejudices that have been thought to justify their subordinate place in the church from the beginning. Though they are a majority of the active members of churches they have until recently been denied positions in decision-making bodies on all levels in the major denominations. Many of the current disabilities of women are in the process of being overcome as a result of pressure by women themselves in church and state, in academic life, in business and industry. The obstacles that remain are great and pressure is still needed.

Although, as I have said, I only recently discovered the importance of this issue, as a teacher I have been troubled for many years by the injustices, frustrations, and waste of talent that I have observed in the case of so many women students. Often they have been the best students, a fact that would have surprised Augustine, Thomas Aquinas, Luther, and many other great Christian men. But after graduation they have been unable to find suitable jobs either in the church or in academic institutions. They have had to accept marginal positions, often on a short-term basis, and usually as assistants to men.

I have been helped to become more aware of the depth of the problem by a group of women in the Graduate Theological Union in Berkeley who are studying the history and theology of the status of women. They are part of an informal national network of women working on these issues. Many theological schools have a policy of encouraging the admission of women as students and slowly they are finding places on faculties. It remains to be seen what the effect of this ferment in the theological schools will be on the churches. I hope that we shall soon see great changes in attitudes and policies.

Women generally get their status in relation to men. The story of the creation of woman from Adam's rib, according to the familiar King James Version, as a "help meet" for man (RSV, "a helper fit for him") has been one source of the subordination of women. There has been enormous exegetical attention to that passage, and there is a tendency now to reverse the earlier impression that it has made. Karl Barth, whose thought at other points tries to combine the idea of equality of men and women with the idea that man is first *in order,* hence the leader, emphasizes the interpretation that woman, who was created last, was the crown of creation. The most important counteracting idea is that the word "help" in the phrase "a help meet for him" refers to a very superior form of help, including divine help, and "does not imply inferiority."[2] The New English Bible reflects this idea in the use of the word "partner" as the translation. What a difference that makes!

Jesus transcended his own culture, including his religious tradition, in his own attitude toward women. He set an example of treating both men and women with equal respect as persons. My recollection is that years ago I was always troubled by Luke's story about Mary and Martha because it seemed to me that Jesus was strangely unfair to Martha. Now I discover that this story is seen as emancipating for women because it gives them a choice between two roles, and it is seen as a departure from custom in giving women the opportunity to receive religious teaching.

Paul has a great deal of responsibility for the continuous teaching in the church that women should have a subordinate role. One example of this is the way in which Dietrich Bonhoeffer in his prison letters, which in so many respects have been emancipating, harks back to Paul's injunction about a woman's obedience to her husband. In a "wedding sermon" which he wrote in his cell and sent to his friend Eberhard Bethge at the time of his marriage to Bonhoeffer's niece, he quotes Paul's words in Colossians: "Wives, be subject to your husbands, as is fitting in the Lord. Husbands, love your wives" (Col. 3:18–19). Then Bonhoeffer adds: "You may order your home as you like, except in one thing: the wife is to be subject to her husband and the husband is to love his wife. In this way God gives to husband and wife the honour that is due to each. The wife's honour is to serve the husband, to be a 'help-meet for him.' " The way in which Bonhoeffer says this and the occasion on which he says it suggest to me that he was not merely repeating some familiar words of Scripture in a perfunctory way but that he was expressing a firm conviction about which he had done fresh thinking in connection with his own engagement.[3]

Paul's various passages about the subordination of women are so familiar that I need not quote many of them. One of his sentences today strikes the reader as curious and not merely wrong. After he says that women should be silent in church, he adds the following: "If there is something they want to know, they can ask their own husbands at home" (I Cor. 14:35, NEB). This assumption of such dependable male wisdom strikes us today as amusing. When sentences that represent this side of Paul, including the statement that "the head of a woman is her husband," are read in public I find that people sometimes laugh. How long have congregations laughed at the reading of Holy Scripture? For how many centuries have the assumptions of those passages been so conveyed to congregations that they have taken their truth for granted?

Today much of the writing about this subject is devoted to the idea that Paul had another side, which these passages do not represent. I believe that this is true and important. If all that Paul had to say on this subject happened to be equally time-bound, that would not make it authoritative for us. It is fortunate that we have passages in Paul's writings that seem to transcend not only Paul's time but even Paul himself.

It is fascinating to find one of these glimpses of new under-standings embedded in one of the most troublesome of Paul's passages about women. After saying that the head of a woman is her husband and that "man was not made from woman, but woman from man" (I Cor. 11:8), he suddenly says: "And yet, in Christ's fellowship woman is as essential to man as man to woman. If woman was made out of man, it is through woman that man now comes to be; and God is the source of all" (I Cor. 11:11–12, NEB). This is a good empirical correction of the Adam-Eve sequence. Some verses are surely more inspired than others. Krister Stendahl regards the great passage in Gal. 3:28 as a "breakthrough": "There is no such thing as Jew and Greek, slave and freeman, male and female; for you are all one person in Christ Jesus" (NEB). He argues against those who neutralize the emancipating implications of the passage by insisting that it does not apply to this world or to the church now but only to the eschatologi-cal status of male and female, as of slave and freeman, before God. He sees in Paul's words "pointers toward a future devel-opment," warning that Paul's words should not be explained away today by taking the actual situation in the first-century church as a norm for all time. Actually the slave-freeman contrast was treated in that way for centuries, but the church found the full truth in the words when in its experience it transcended that limiting interpretation. The same process is now taking place in regard to the male-female contrast.[4]

There is also the remarkable element of mutuality in the relations between men and women that is enjoined by Paul in I Cor. 7:4. In the midst of a discussion that is for the most part negative about marriage and is conditioned by Paul's expectation of an early end of history, there is this statement: "The wife does not rule over her own body, but the husband does; likewise the husband does not rule over his own body, but the wife does." The remarkable thing about this passage is that it does stress mutuality and not a one-sided control by the man. A recent study of woman in medieval theology by Eleanor McLaughlin, a scholar who is a radical critic of the tradition, calls this "a truly revolutionary concept." She .shows that in the theology of Thomas Aquinas this mutuality was greatly reduced by the exceptions that he admitted. She says: "There is clearly a conflict between the Christian view of sexual reciprocity and medieval society's deeply held belief that a man belongs to himself and a woman belongs to a man." But she says that tension between the two never disappeared, and that "the capitulation is not complete."[5]

When one reads about the prevailing attitudes toward women and toward sex in other periods, one wonders if one is reading about the same religion to which one is committed today. The idea that sex was inherently a sinful thing and the blaming of that sin on women by solemn theologians for centuries made for one of the most unlovely chapters in Christian history.

Now it is taken for granted that sexual relations are not evil in themselves but can express a deeply personal relationship. Current discussion of marriage emphasizes the two ends of marriage—procreation and mutual love. The crudely negative teaching about women has fortunately been abandoned. Both Catholic and Protestant teaching greatly emphasizes the family in the most positive way. Both virginity and motherhood have been exalted in all periods, but Protestants have never exalted the former, and Catholics today, with Protestants, give emphasis to the latter.

One interesting chapter in recent Protestant thought was the teaching of such representatives of the liberal social gospel as Walter Rauschenbusch and Lyman Abbott. Abbott did not even believe in women's suffrage. In a book entitled *The*

Homebuilder published in 1908 he glorifies woman's role in private life as the mother of many children. He says of the "homebuilder" that she "believes in woman's rights, and she thinks that among them is the right to be exempt from militia duty, police duty, jury duty—and suffrage duty." Walter Rauschenbusch did believe in women's suffrage, but he believed that the proper role of women was that of wife and mother in a family consecrated by the presence of quite a few children, and he lacked sympathy for other careers for women.[6] As an example of the thinking of the period, President Grover Cleveland wrote an article in the *Ladies' Home Journal* in 1905 in which he furiously attacked women's clubs and said that "the best and safest club for a woman to patronize is her home." He also opposed the movement for women's suffrage and said that such participation by women in public affairs would have "a dangerous and undermining effect on the characters of the wives and mothers of the land." Those words, which belong to this century, seem to come from a strange world.[7]

This tendency to define the role of women chiefly in terms of motherhood is often beautifully expressed by contemporary theologians and by the pope. It does not necessarily imply inferiority or subjection. Men and women may be regarded as equal, but having different functions. Clearly this is an important part of the truth, and advocates of the liberation of women who give little or no emphasis to it are unwise. Giving birth to children and taking major responsibility for their nurture during their most formative years are obviously unique and indispensable forms of creativity. Yet this exaltation of motherhood as the most characteristic function of women can be a trap for them, especially under present conditions.

The most important reason for this is that women usually do not have and will not have the large number of children that at one time made the family a considerable community for which to have major responsibility. If there are only two children, motherhood is far from being a lifework. A mother can often look forward to forty years after her children cease to need from her anything like full-time care. I think that failure to realize the implications of this great change is the greatest obstacle to an understanding of why conventional ideas about the role of a woman as mother, no matter how exalted that role is, are inadequate. In the past, the wife and mother in a large family had a commanding role that made use of a great variety of gifts of mind and spirit for many years. Caring for children was combined with much educating and administering, acting as hostess, diplomat, financial manager, and first aid expert on many things for a large circle of family and friends.

Dorothy Sayers as long ago as 1938 observed that, for many women, this kind of home was no longer a reality. She wrote as follows:

> The fact remains that the home contains much less of interesting activity than it used to contain. What is more, the home has so shrunk to the size of a small flat that— even if we restrict woman's job to the bearing and rearing of families—there is no room for her to do even that. It is useless to urge the modern woman to have twelve children, like her grandmother. Where is she to put them when she has got them? And what modern man wants to be bothered with them? It is perfectly idiotic to take away women's traditional occupations and then complain because she looks for new ones. Every woman is a human being—one cannot repeat that too often— and a human being *must* have occupation, if he or she is not to become a nuisance to the world.[8]

The pattern has changed in another respect. After a long struggle women now have the opportunity to go to college, to do advanced graduate work, and to be trained for professions. They know that they have the intellectual capacities and creative gifts that are important outside the family circle. The limited period of the most demanding family responsibilities, especially when combined with parental mutuality, frees them to make other contributions from which society will benefit and from which their lives will gain in significance and fulfillment. For women to be able to look forward only to years of routine jobs as assistants to men is a loss both to society and to themselves.

The practical problems that arise in these changing patterns of life are many and baffling. These problems often create strains in marriages and lead to many divorces. For example, when both husband and wife are prepared to take jobs they must decide whether they will live where the husband has his best opportunity for employment or where the wife has hers. A short time ago that was not an open question, as it was taken for granted that the husband's job had the priority. Now this is no longer taken for granted. A new generation is already living with that and similar difficult problems.

I have an impression, more from what is not said than from what is said, that those who make the liberation of women their chief cause suggest that the better role for women must always be a public role; paid jobs are always better than voluntary forms of participation in church and community. The idea that sometimes a woman might choose to make her contribution through her husband's work when that is congenial may seem to some a case of retrogression. I may have no right to an opinion as a man, but it seems to me that the objective of women's liberation should not be to encourage women to follow only one or two new paths; the objective should be to enable women and men to have freedom to choose between many options against the background of newly achieved equality of status and dignity.

Another dimension of the present struggle of women for full personhood is the overcoming of sexist one-sidedness in the symbols of faith, theology, and worship. The tendency to think of God as male and not as inclusive being—beyond sexual differentiation—is pervasive. This tendency is encour-

aged by the language that is always used in liturgies. The use
of "man" as the generic word for humanity (which includes
both men and women) is not free from sexist one-sidedness,
regardless of the intention. The use of masculine pronouns at
nearly every point when we speak of God in theological
discourse or in prayers and hymns is such a habit that those
who have been accustomed to it for decades seldom think
about it. A younger generation of women is asking why this
should be. I know many younger women who feel that everything about the worship of the church leaves them out and
they wonder if they can take it much longer. Many others
have already dropped out of church for this reason. Even
when men make an effort to be contemporary and prepare
liturgies with many references to the achievements and the
sufferings of the present, it is my experience that women are
generally omitted. I grant that there are rhetorical difficulties in finding inclusive nouns or pronouns. It is embarrass-
ingly difficult to find hymns that are wholly satisfactory.

This concern about the need of changing the language
about God and humanity is not limited to a few outspoken
"feminists." Denominations are beginning to discuss ways of
revising language used in liturgies, educational materials,
and official documents. In June 1974 the most widely representative group of women that has ever met under the auspices of the church was convened in West Berlin by the
World Council of Churches. Every part of the world and
every major tradition in the constituency of the World Council was represented. The recommendations of this conference greatly stressed the need to study "God-language" as
used in the churches. It suggested, among other things, that
committees responsible for Bible translation be asked to correct "sexist errors" in translations. They had in view the
whole range of concerns involved in the struggle for equal
status for women. It is of special interest to note that this
conference was regarded as rather conservative by some of
the American delegates. Surely the problem of theological

and liturgical language lies at the heart of the life of all churches.

Because of their traditions, polities, and habits, the churches must bear a large part of the responsibility for the male chauvinism of our culture. They are now beginning to realize that they have a special obligation to counteract the destructive effects of their own past.

BLACK THEOLOGY OF LIBERATION

James Cone is the chief systematic exponent of a "black theology" of liberation. He states one reason for a new black theology: "No white theologian has ever taken the oppression of black people as a point of departure for analyzing God's activity in contemporary America."[9] I am sure he is right. One could say more than that: The predominantly white churches and their white theologians did not face the full depth of the wrong done by our country to blacks since its beginning until after they were prodded by a new generation of blacks in the 1950's.

As critics look back upon the theologians of the social gospel movement they charge them with neglecting the problem of black oppression, with showing almost no awareness of what was happening to blacks in their own time. This was true of Walter Rauschenbusch, the greatest of them. In the case of Josiah Strong, one of the most popular writers connected with the movement, there was a tendency to think of the global supremacy of Anglo-Saxons. Strong was also concerned about the effect of the great influx of non-Anglo-Saxon immigrants upon our cities. This was a kind of racism that is shocking to us, but it was congenial to the flamboyant belief in world progress under the leadership of "advanced" peoples that was common in the "progressive era" around 1900.

Explanations of this neglect in the case of many leaders of the social gospel include the idea that they were Northerners who regarded oppression of blacks as a Southern problem. Their culture-affirming optimism kept them from perceiving the malignancy and pervasiveness of this evil in their culture.[10]

I have been surprised in rereading my first book, *Social Salvation*, in which I dealt with many social evils that had priority for me in 1935, that the evil of racial injustice was not one of them. I was concerned chiefly about the human consequences of the economic depression and about the threat of war.

Rauschenbusch and others were aware of the horror of episodes of lynching and he included them as one of the marks of "the Kingdom of Evil." He traced the origin of the lynching spirit to "our fathers" who "created the conditions of sin by the African slave trade and by the unearned wealth they gathered from slave labour for generations."[11]

One major reason for the neglect of black oppression was preoccupation with economic issues. Racial injustice has a most important economic aspect, but what concerned Rauschenbusch and his generation was the rapacity of untamed business, the lack of power of the industrial workers, and the poverty in Northern cities, which they knew firsthand. My book was a case in point. While that is no defense of my own limited awareness, it does give some explanation of my priorities at the time.

The famous "Social Creed of the Churches," adopted by the Federal Council of Churches in 1908, dealt only with economic issues and did not mention race. It is more remarkable that when the creed was expanded and revised in 1932 there was the same neglect of race. That expanded statement began: "The Churches Should Stand For:" There followed seventeen articles, thirteen of which dealt with economic objectives. One dealt with the treatment of offenders; another with the repudiation of war, calling for the peaceable settlement of all controversies; a third dealt with freedom of speech and assembly and the press and freedom of communication of mind with mind. There was also the following article: "Justice, opportunity and equal rights for all; mutual goodwill and cooperation among racial, economic and religious groups." This was the only reference to race in a document that was called "The Social Ideals of the Churches" and that, after four years of preparation, was adopted by a full meeting of the representatives of the denominations that were members of the Federal Council of Churches—in matters of social policy the chief predecessor of the National Council of Churches.

I want to put beside that total neglect of the oppression of black Americans the testimony of one of the most admired black leaders of the last generation, Dr. Benjamin E. Mays, president for many years of Morehouse College. Dr. Mays is not a militant, and he is quite free from the more recent antiwhite attitudes. Indeed I would be surprised if he did not have great difficulty with the idea of "black theology." Yet in his autobiography entitled *Born to Rebel* (1971) he describes the plight of black people before and after the appearance of that statement of "The Social Ideals of the Churches" in words that are as devastating in their criticism of white oppressors as any the most militant blacks use today. He writes as follows: "Not only in major areas the right to vote, the right to economic security, the right to education, the right to decent housing—was the Negro deprived. But these basic denials proliferated also in countless ways to guarantee that every Negro should be consistently subjected to humiliating injustices and insults calculated to destroy his self-respect, his pride, and his sense of manhood."[12] This moderate leader, who was himself highly honored by the churches, having been a vice-president of the Federal Council of Churches in 1948, and who late in life became president of the Atlanta Board of Education, makes this judgment about the churches: "I believe that throughout my lifetime, the local white church has been society's most conservative and hypocritical institution in the area of White-Negro relations."[13]

Such words from a contemporary militant might be regarded as coming out of hostility toward the white church, but Benjamin Mays has no such hostility. His book is full of reports of experiences that he himself suffered that illustrate all that he says about the systematic efforts to humiliate his race. It is out of this bitter experience that black theology has come. White people have nothing in their experience that enables them fully to understand it. Martin Luther King, Jr., who embodied all that was most persuasive in the civil rights movement, did more than anyone else to bring about a change in the outlook of a great many persons in the white churches. He had trouble until the very end with the idea of "black power," even though he organized black power with great effect. I doubt if he would ever have chosen to put together the words "black theology." Yet without that early civil rights movement which he represented, I wonder if black theology today would not be an unheeded voice in a white wilderness.

I realize that many readers may regard this as a one-sided picture of the role of white people both in the North and in the South between the 1920's and the 1950's. There were many efforts to deal with specific issues as they arose. For example, it was the practice of church groups to avoid meeting in any place where there might be discrimination against blacks, and this was a matter of great symbolic importance. There were also pioneering activities by many institutions, such as the student Christian movements and especially the Y.W.C.A., in arranging interracial events. White leaders in the North gave strong support to the Fellowship (later Committee) of Southern Churchmen, which was involved in considerable costly pioneering in the South. Much spadework was done by Southern moderates to counteract the venom of race prejudice. This side of the story, however, does not cancel out the massive support by most churches of discrimination against and segregation of the black minority.

A leading African theologian, John Mbiti, a professor from

Uganda who is now the director of the Ecumenical Institute of the World Council of Churches, has warned that black theology is an American phenomenon and not representative of black Africa. He says: "It was forced into existence by the particularities of American history." He says that in southern Africa black theology deserves a hearing. But he makes the interesting comment that blacks in southern Africa, unlike those in the United States, are not free to *talk* about black liberation; they need first to be liberated. He says that African theology "grows out of our joy in the experience of the Christian faith, whereas Black theology emerges from the pains of oppression." This also must be a partial view because there is oppression in black Africa, not least in Mbiti's own country, Uganda, where it is often oppression of blacks by blacks. Mbiti does not deny the validity of black theology in the United States and he does underline its special strategic role here.[14]

Black theology belongs to the stage of the black struggle for liberation that has followed the early spring of the civil rights movement when it was a cause with clear objectives that aroused great enthusiasm in the white liberal community both religious and secular. During that period many gains were made in overcoming legal barriers to desegregation and also in enabling blacks to secure the right to vote where it had been denied them, a right that they have used. The political power that blacks are gaining now may well be the most important result of the legislation passed in that period.

Black theology belongs to a later period, one in which blacks are disillusioned about the substance of the early gains, in which integration is seen as token entrance into the white world on terms set by whites, in which voluntary separatism in place of imposed segregation has considerable attraction. The gains of the civil rights movement created more hopeful changes in the South than in the North. The Northern backlash against efforts to integrate schools be-

came as ugly and as stubborn as the earlier Southern backlash. The most frustrating aspect of the continuing oppression of blacks is in the increase of the economic deprivation
of the majority of them. Urban ghetto communities are
cursed by unemployment rates of 30 to 40 percent of their
young people, and the national rate of black unemployment
is more than double that of whites. Also, the gap between
incomes of blacks and whites has widened even though many
blacks with training have better opportunities than before.
Many cities have black mayors, but too often their task is to
preside over urban deterioration and inhuman conditions for
their own race. On the other side I think it should be said that
the efforts of educational institutions on all levels to include
blacks and to counteract the effects of their exclusion from
educational opportunities in the past has been considerable.
Also, there is much less of the deliberate humiliation of black
people by the white majority in both North and South.

I confess it is difficult for me as a white man to write about
black theology. I am in danger of doing one of two things in
any given case. It is easy to say an uncritical "yes" to all that
is said against white people, out of a sense of guilt for the past.
It is also easy to become defensive against what may seem to
be unfair attacks upon whites. If I were to follow James
Cone's advice literally, I would be silent on the subject. He
says: "If whites were really serious about their radicalism in
regard to the black revolution and its theological implications in America, they would keep silent and take instruc-
tions from black people."[15] Yet if I were to write about other
movements for liberation and neglect black liberation, this
would suggest indifference, a sure sign of white racism.

Both white and black critics may think that I give too much
attention to James Cone's version of black theology, which
they may be inclined to regard as an ephemeral explosion. I
do not doubt that it, like most white theologies, will soon be
dated. But Cone is the most systematic black theologian today and his thought is reflected in corporate statements of

the National Committee of Black Churchmen. It is taken seriously by Gayraud S. Wilmore, author of the recent and much-admired comprehensive statement of black religious thinking, *Black Religion and Black Radicalism* (Doubleday, 1972).

Cone's black theology at its center is an affirmation of the liberating work of God for all oppressed peoples. The exodus is seen as the original liberating event, which reveals that God "is the God of the oppressed, involved in their history, liberating them from bondage."[16] Cone says: "The resurrection event means that God's liberating work is not only for the house of Israel but for all who are enslaved by the principalities and powers."[17] Cone regards his theology as centered in Jesus Christ and he stresses as I have done the identification of Christ with the poor and oppressed. He begins his first book, *Black Theology and Black Power*, by saying that "Black Power" is "Christ's central message to twentieth century America."[18] He comes to this conclusion because faithfulness to Jesus Christ as the liberator of black people requires, in his view, the use of black power to effect that liberation. He has no patience at all with those who draw pacifist implications from the teachings of Jesus. He is disdainful of white people who preach nonviolence to black people while in their own interests they control the many forms of institutionalized coercion or violence that keep blacks in their position of inferiority and deprivation. I have no quarrel with the conclusion that faithfulness to Jesus Christ does not involve a law of nonviolence applicable to all situations, but I think that Cone too easily reduces the tension between violence and the teachings of Jesus; however, I am more interested in emphasizing that tension in addressing oppressors than I am in addressing the oppressed. Cone speaks much of Christ as black or as a black event. He says that "thinking of Christ as non-black in the twentieth century is as theologically impossible as thinking of him as non-Jewish in the first century."[19] He is using "black" symbolically and not literally as, I think, Albert Cleage, Jr., does in his book *The Black Messiah*.[20]

The casual reader can be thrown off by Cone's use of the words "black" and "white." He is responsible for a natural misinterpretation because he does not explain what he is doing with the words except in two footnotes in *A Black Theology of Liberation*.[21] I think that he must intentionally preserve this ambiguity because he wants all white people, in the first instance at least, to feel the lash of his rhetoric against whiteness as such. And he wants to keep the emphasis on those who are literally black because they are the largest oppressed community in the United States.

In his footnotes Cone does say that "white" may refer to an attitude rather than to a color in the literal sense. He is aware that after his wholesale criticism of all white theology he may be taunted for depending as much as he does on Karl Barth and Paul Tillich. Also, "black" may refer to all suffering and oppressed people. Cone does speak of this in the text of his book (pp. 27, 28). This would be his answer to those who wonder where the Indians and the Chicanos and impoverished and oppressed white people come in. It would be his answer also in the ecumenical context to those who wonder at the provincialism of his books in their neglect of yellow and brown peoples. Had Cone been more careful about this use of words, his books might too quickly have provided an "out" for his white readers; attention might have been so diverted toward a global context for liberation that the intensity of his concern for the black victims of American white people would have been lost. The following two sentences represent many others: "American white theology is a theology of the Antichrist, insofar as it arises from an identification with the white community, thereby placing God's approval on white oppression of black existence."[22] The words "insofar as" enable Cone to make exceptions, though he would not want this to become a habit. "He [God] is not color blind in the black-white struggle, but has made an unqualified identification with black people."[23]

The narrowness of Cone's focus may be seen in the way in which he deals with the Vietnam war. He questions the "authenticity" of the white opposition to the war, since "the destruction of black humanity began long before the Vietnam war and few white people got upset about it."[24] He asks: "Is it because white boys are dying in the war that whites get so upset?" The direct, deliberate, and massive destruction of Vietnamese, who are not white, by our Government was not paralleled by comparable direct, deliberate, and massive destruction of blacks by our Government. There was an emergency aspect of the officially initiated and guided destruction in Vietnam that makes Cone's remarks on this subject an indication of a blind spot of his own. Also, there was a disproportionate use of American blacks in the war because of the deferments that were readily open to many more whites. They were sent to kill yellow people and became victims themselves. I was always sorry that more black leaders did not share the outrage of Martin Luther King, Jr., about the war, for—in spite of all inherited deprivations and handicaps—articulate blacks could have had considerable influence on public opinion and on the Federal Government.

All theologies are to some extent strategic theologies. They give emphasis to the questions of a particular time and place and they seek to counteract what are believed to be the errors that are most tempting at the time of writing. Cone's black theology is so much a strategic theology that, especially in its doctrine of sin, it will surely be misleading as new situations develop. In the context of this book at this time I understand his statement, "Because sin is a concept that is meaningful only for an oppressed community as it reflects on liberation, it is not possible to make a universal analysis that is meaningful for both black and white people."[25] The strategic nature of this theology is seen in his statement that while black theology does not deny that all men are sinners, "what it denies is white reflections on the sin of black people."[26] I am not interested in white reflections on the sin of black people. I do think that it is important that black theology show some signs that it is preparing black people for the discovery of their own sins, for their own self-criticism. I fail to see that this is yet one of Cone's interests. His use of "white," ambiguous as it is, according to two footnotes, does easily give the impression that the destruction of white sources of sin and error would liberate all humanity. Such a sentence as the following may easily mislead whites and blacks alike: "What we need is the destruction of whiteness, which is the source of human misery in the world."[27] I think that it would be good if Cone were to put a theological message in a sealed envelope to be read at some future time when black people gain more power, when blacks are seen to be oppressors of other blacks or of whites. This is especially important because black theology is a call to revolution, and revolutionaries, whatever form the revolution may take, are greatly tempted to a passionate self-righteousness which distorts the mind and the spirit. I am not concerned about threats of black violence that Cone engages in, because I agree with him that the greater violence today is the violence of "the system" against blacks.

I think that there is an element of unreality in Cone's tendency to regard white racism as monolithic and unchanging with all whites save those who are "black" in spirit. I realize that it is easier to see this element of unreality when one sees the world from a white perspective, and I cannot avoid doing that. Cone's writings are intended to be polemical, and he paints with a broad brush, but it would be desirable to relate black theology to a more empirical effort to diagnose the phenomenon of racism. I am not the one to do that, but there are a few considerations that I should like to raise for discussion. This is a racist culture. Racism is embedded in institutions as varied as racially slanted intelligence tests, the habits of police, and practices in the sale of real estate. The deposit of centuries of an imposed state of inferiority has left its mark on what black people expect for themselves and on what white people expect of them.

Some results of a Harris poll taken among American blacks show the terrible consequences that remain of the centuries of oppression. "More than four out of five blacks think that whites consider Negroes inferior. Two thirds of blacks believe whites to be afraid that blacks are better people than they are. Nearly the same number—63%—feel that whites regret having abolished slavery." (*Time*, April 6, 1970.) That last statement I find incredible, but even if it is exaggerated it reveals a great deal about what blacks see as present-day racism.

Yet there have been significant changes in law, and to a considerable extent law has been an educator. Blacks in the South, as I have said, seem now to be more hopeful than are blacks in the North. For this both federal law and Southern black power have a good deal of the responsibility. The old-fashioned political racist demagogues are dying out and the constituency to which they have appealed is narrowing. The election of black sheriffs in Southern counties is regarded as having special importance for the day-to-day welfare of black people. I think that the election by a whole state of high black officials such as Wilson Riles, the chief education officer of California, is a sign of the diminution of prejudice. Also, fortunate blacks who are well trained are in great demand for employment by many institutions, including universities, church bureaucracies, and private business. However, I should not do much celebrating of gains for blacks until the walls that surround ghettos are leveled and until the statistics concerning black unemployment and black incomes change radically for the better.

If we think of conscious attitudes of white people, it seems to me that more emphasis should be put on diversity. There is a wide spectrum of attitudes. On the one hand there are the hostile racists who seek to keep blacks in positions of inferiority. On the other hand there are those who tend to treat blacks as objects, or who show awkwardness in their relations with them, but who sincerely support black causes. If you call the latter group "racists," it makes a difference that on most issues they can be persuaded to be allies of black power and that their votes add up as well as black votes. Black liberation depends on black power, but not on isolated black power. It must have allies, but Cone's polemics leave little space for them.

Also, it should be recognized that many whites are first- or second-generation Americans and their ancestors had no part in the slave system or in the establishment and hardening of the institutions of discrimination and segregation. Often they were Europe's poor, and they are not won to the black cause by rhetoric that associates them with those sins of American history. The language of reparations, while justified in many contexts, makes little sense to them. Today they should be helped to see that it is superficial for them to compare their winning of their way as white people in spite of initial ethnic disadvantages in this country with the situation of blacks who have handicaps growing out of centuries of an imposed status of inferiority. There is here a human problem that is not helped by wholesale denunciations.

The tension between blacks and Jews, seen in the issue of quotas, in confrontations in the ghetto between blacks and Jews (the latter as landlords, shopkeepers, teachers, and social workers), and in the common black identification with Arabs as part of the Third World, is one of the most tragic aspects of the racial conflict in America. This is a unique problem in itself and calls for careful thought. It is not helped by undiscriminating polemics based upon our nation's history of black oppression.

Cone would regard it as a diversion, but I think that in the long run we should see the white American attitude toward blacks as part of a more comprehensive racism that does not easily accept the humanity of nonwhite people on other continents. It is not a static attitude. We have seen the Japanese become accepted as human after they were hated as subhuman yellow creatures during the Second World War. The Chinese, who were "yellow hordes" for so long, are much admired for their achievements in transforming their country. I hope that a similar change will come in the American attitude toward the people of Indochina, whose racial difference made it possible for Americans to treat them as "gooks" who could easily be made victims of atrocities on land and targets of relentless bombing from the air. I have referred to an Anglo-Saxon and northern European racism that has in the past controlled the attitude of Americans to "lesser breeds without the Law." It dominated immigration policies until recently. It is no longer often defended, but it remains a strong influence and clouds the vision of large parts of the population.

I have no zeal for these criticisms of Cone's black theology because I believe that it appeared at the right time and that it has important work to do. It has deepened my own awareness of the blind spots of white theologians, beginning with myself.

THE LIBERATION THEOLOGY
OF GUSTAVO GUTIERREZ

I shall now discuss the most fully developed theology of liberation, a Latin-American product. I shall limit myself to the thought of the Peruvian Roman Catholic theologian, Gustavo Gutiérrez. Latin America is that part of the "Third World" which has been strongly influenced by the Christian traditions. The only exception is the Republic of the Philippines, which has a similar Spanish Roman Catholic background. In ecumenical theological discussions Latin Americans, both Catholic and Protestant, are the most articulate representatives of a revolutionary theology of liberation. I do not claim that they speak for the whole Third World, but they make a case for the need of radical change, a case that is applicable to many other Third World countries, and their resistance to the power of Western and northern hemisphere capitalism and imperialism is very widely shared. I sometimes hear the criticism that Americans should not give great attention to this latest theology from abroad but should look to the theological impulses that come from the American experience. I do not quarrel with those who do seek theological inspiration and models in the United States, but I have several reasons for emphasizing this Latin-American theology of liberation at this time.

The first reason is that together with the considerable social awakening in the Catholic Church, from such bishops as Cardinal Silva in Chile and Archbishop Câmara in Brazil to a large company of priests and lay people who are committed to the struggle for radical change, this theology is an expression of an extraordinary religious transformation. Latin-American Catholicism as recently as fifteen or twenty years ago was widely regarded as an almost hopeless segment of the Christian church. It was closely allied with the dominant political and social powers. It represented in an extreme form theological obscurantism and religious intolerance. Protestants regarded the church in many countries of Latin America as a persecuting church and the laws that suppressed the freedom of religious minorities in some countries were among the worst in the world. In recent years the changes, it seems to me, are a miracle of the spirit, changes concerning matters of religious liberty, the development of an open theology, and the social teaching and commitment of a large part of the church.

I have already referred in Chapter IV to the remarkable defense of human rights by national hierarchies in Latin America. On social and economic issues radical Christians find a source of support, or at least a point of departure, both in Pope Paul's encyclical *Populorum Progressio* and in the report of the conference of the whole hierarchy of Latin America that met in Medellín, Colombia, in 1968. That report is often said to be in advance of the personal views of a majority of the bishops, many of whom were prodded by their advisors. They were influenced by the pope and by the pressures of the situation. However that may be, the Medellín documents are an important support for those who take a socially progressive, even radical position. In his book *A Theology of Liberation* Gutiérrez uses them in that way.[28] My first point is that this extraordinary change in one part of the worldwide church is part of the history of the whole church and should be an inspiration to both Catholics and Protestants in the United States.

My second reason for emphasizing the Latin-American form of the theology of liberation is that especially in the work of Gutiérrez it offers us a strong theological position that comes out of a particular situation that has meaning for us all. It is well grounded Biblically and is based on broad learning in theology. It is sometimes criticized for being too much an importation from Germany and not sufficiently indigenous. I do not see that this is a criticism. Gutiérrez's knowledge of progressive German Protestant and Catholic theology has given him freedom from Spanish forms of Catholicism and more broadly from Catholic scholasticism. He has used his German sources for his own purpose. What he has produced is no mere echo of European or any other foreign theology.

He does not give us a total theological system but a theological stance. He has developed insights that are most important for the guidance of those who are in the social struggle for liberation. My personal interest in Gutiérrez stems from my belief that he gives us who have been influenced by various American social theologies, by residues of the social gospel or by Christian realism, a new inspiration and a new theological vision that corrects some of the limitations of both and yet intensifies the social concern that both expressed. It is a strategic theology and not any final theological word. But, as I have said, I believe that theologies are generally strategic, designed to correct the limitations of the present mind of the church and to illumine the experience of their place and time. It is one of Gutiérrez's first principles that theology is "critical reflection on *praxis*," and not a deduction from a given system of thought.

My third reason for emphasizing this expression of liberation theology, coming as it does out of a situation that may seem remote from North American experience, is that the situation in Latin America is of enormous importance for North American experience. Awareness of it fills out most significantly our awareness of the contemporary human condition in a small world. Also, and more important, this theology has a direct message to the United States and especially to Christians here because of the effect of the power of the United States on the people of Latin America. The situation out of which Gutiérrez writes belongs to the North American situation because it is so much influenced by decisions made by our Government and by our corporations. Gutiérrez greatly emphasizes this fact. For example, he addresses the following words to us in the north: "Among more alert groups today, what we have called a new awareness of Latin American reality is making headway. They believe that there can be authentic development for Latin America only if there is liberation from the domination exercised by the great capitalist countries, and especially by the most powerful, the United States of America."[29]

I have gone into this explanation of my use of *A Theology of Liberation* by Gustavo Gutiérrez because of criticism to the effect that, as usual, American theologians are latching on to one more fad or one more foreign thinker! I shall now comment on a few of the ideas in this book that are most important to me.

I have already mentioned Gutiérrez's basic view of theological method. It is a critical reflection on experience, always in the light of the normative sources of Christian faith. This principle is an emancipating one for Gutiérrez, but I think that he regards it as more original than it is. Much Protestant theology is critical reflection on experience, from Luther to Schleiermacher and beyond. Most American theology has been critical reflection on experience. Certainly that was true of Walter Rauschenbusch, who was led to his main emphasis by his experience as a pastor in the slums of New York, and of Reinhold Niebuhr, who was very much influenced both by his experience as a pastor of the social injustice and the power struggles in Detroit and by his continuous response to social situations and political choices.

Gutiérrez, as much as any Christian thinker of whom I know, is shaken by his awareness of a reality that most white Christian thinkers in the United States know about intellectually but not in a way that causes them to be shaken. He puts it in this way: "It is only in the last few years that people have become clearly aware of the scope of misery, and especially of the oppressive and alienating circumstances in which the great majority of mankind exists. Moreover, today people are more deeply aware both of personal responsibility for this situation, and the obstacles these conditions present to the complete fulfillment of all men, exploiters and exploited alike."[30]

Why has this unsettling reality so recently entered our consciousness? I suggest three reasons for it. First, during the period of imperialistic control of most of humanity by Western white powers, there was a lack of concern for the poor even in the imperial nations themselves. This was true until the poor in those nations began to gain power. There was even less concern for the poor of different races and cultures at a great distance. Those who did have some concern were optimistic believers who had confidence that the advance of civilization would put things right or that the spread of Christianity would of itself lift the level of life of the world's majority and provide them with the opportunity of becoming more like their Western masters.

A second reason is obviously the extraordinary development of communication. Today we frequently see starving people on our television screens. I have just read a long article in one of our best newspapers about the conditions under which large numbers of people are living in Calcutta. It is especially about their hunger, and it is written with both realism and compassion. Though I put this picture out of my mind most of the time, I cannot avoid being haunted by it frequently. These are the kinds of experience that we have almost daily. I do not know how much our multitude of travelers abroad see these conditions, but travel is also a factor.

A third reason is the articulateness of the people in the new nations and among the poor everywhere. Also their power is growing. Sometimes it is power to check the power of those who have the wealth, but more often it is power to cause anxiety concerning "stability" in the world. One of the constructive roles of Communism has been that it offers an alternative to poor and oppressed people that can at least be a bargaining point with oppressors. This has caused both wars and repressions out of fear of the advance of Communism, and much misery has come from it. Yet the existence of that alternative has done much to create concern about the misery of the majority. I do not know a theologian who has worked this relatively new understanding of the misery of the majority of the world's people into his theology with better effect than Gutiérrez.

Gutiérrez regularly contrasts the idea of *liberation* with that of *development*. Long before I read his book I was present with him at a meeting on "the theology of development" in 1969 near Geneva. It was Gutiérrez who first made me realize the inadequacy of the idea of development as it was generally used in ecumenical circles. Development was seen by him to be a concept imposed by the so-called "developed" nations upon the others, and it was accompanied by the suggestion that the former were models to be imitated by the so-called "underdeveloped" or "developing" nations.

There was no clear recognition that liberation from domination by the more powerful "developed" nations was essential. There was in addition the tendency to interpret development largely in terms of economic growth and the raising of the standard of living when far more than these were needed and desired.

In contrast to the idea of development Gutiérrez says that liberation is on three levels. The first level "expresses the aspirations of oppressed peoples and social classes, emphasizing the conflictual aspect of the economic, social and political process which puts them at odds with the wealthy nations and oppressive classes." At a deeper level liberation means a new historical consciousness involving the assumption of responsibility by the people themselves for their own destiny. Here belong the preparations to participate in revolutionary activity to make possible what Gutiérrez calls "a new man and a qualitatively better society." At a still deeper level Gutiérrez sees liberation as salvation in the full Christian sense with Christ as the liberator. It is liberation from sin as the ultimate root of injustice and oppression.

Behind much of this exposition is Gutiérrez's dependence on Paulo Freire, the exiled Brazilian educator whose *Pedagogy of the Oppressed* has brought his methods of education to the attention of the whole ecumenical community and beyond.[31] Among other things this is a program of adult education, often of literacy education, that uses materials and methods that enable people to understand the meaning of their present oppressed condition and to see it in contrast to their true humanity. They become aware of their full dignity and of their possibilities. They become prepared to participate in their own liberation, in the political processes, including revolutionary action essential for freedom from their present deprivation, humiliation, and oppression. This is the beginning of spiritual liberation, and without it there can be no political liberation. An educational process that is so distinctive needs to be described by a distinctive word. Freire and others use the word "conscientization." This word is used by Gutiérrez and remarkably it is also used by the Latin-American bishops in the report of their conference at Medellín.

Gutiérrez is Marxist in his acceptance of the class struggle as being both a present reality and the source of revolutionary dynamism. He says: "It is undeniable that the class struggle poses problems to the universality of Christian love and the unity of the Church." Yet he goes on to say: "The class struggle is a fact, and neutrality in this matter is impossible."[32] He is not bound by a dogmatic view of the pattern of classes and says that "the evolution of the class struggle and its exact extent, its nuances, are the object of analysis of the social sciences."[33] It is my impression that he uses Marxism quite freely to illumine his situation very much as Reinhold Niebuhr did in his *Moral Man and Immoral Society* in 1932. Gutiérrez clearly envisages the need of violent revolution in Latin America and looks back to the Cuban revolution as having played a "catalytic role."[34] He does not discuss revolutionary violence at length, but he gives moral permission for it because he sees it as in some cases necessary if the "institutionalized violence" of the oppressive *status quo* is to be overcome.

In all discussions of revolutionary violence in Christian circles in Latin America and elsewhere there is great emphasis on what is called "institutionalized violence," or "systemic violence," or sometimes "covert violence." This is not as visible as what we generally call "violence," the bloody violence of revolutionary action, but it is as lethal, and it is active on a much larger scale. Institutionalized violence that results for generations in the malnutrition of children or in a relatively low life expectancy in society is lethal. This concept of "institutionalized violence" was also stressed by the bishops at Medellín, though they warned against revolutionary violence as likely to bring greater evils. Pope Paul in his *Populorum Progressio*, in one paragraph (para. 31) appears to give permission for revolutionary violence in extremely oppressive circumstances, but he then warns against it on the same ground. In the various reports that have been prepared under the auspices of the World Council of Churches there is this same stress on institutionalized violence and a reluctant admission that revolutionary violence may be a moral necessity. One of the revolutionary Christian heroes in Latin America is Camilo Torres. He came to the conclusion that, even at the expense of separation from the priesthood, he should join a band of guerrillas in Colombia. He died in combat in 1966, and as a result he has become a kind of martyr among those who believe in the role of the violent revolutionary. Archbishop Helder Câmara, while a believer in nonviolence, has emphasized his respect for those who believe that they must choose the way of revolutionary violence. He said: "I feel that the memory of Camilo Torres and Che Guevara merits as much respect as that of Martin Luther King."[35] He also has a salutary warning against becoming "armchair guerrillas."

Gutiérrez sees participation in the class struggle as consistent with universal love. He says that universal love does not mean avoidance of confrontation with oppressors. In the United States when there is a raw conflict on issues of racial justice or on the rights of workers to organize, involvement in social conflict is often seen to be a better expression of love than talk about reconciliation that papers over the issues that divide. Gutiérrez is not saying more than this in principle, but the conflict in which he takes sides is one in which the nature of the total political and economic structures are at stake. He accepts the fact that for him oppressors are enemies. Love for these enemies means that by opposing them, those on the side of the oppressed may liberate them "from their inhuman condition as oppressors."[36] This can be used to rationalize unrestrained violence and terror against opponents. It is not clear to me how Gutiérrez guards against this. Paulo Freire, on whom he depends so much, includes the teaching of such restraint as part of his "pedagogy of the oppressed." Freire writes that "in order for the struggle to have meaning, the oppressed must not, in seeking to regain their humanity (which is a way to create it) become in turn oppressors of the oppressors, but the restorers of the humanity of both."[37]

I realize that readers who live in quite different situations may regard this talk about "oppressed" and "oppressors" as inflammatory rhetoric that really distorts theology and the facts. I think that we have to be situational about this and recognize that if such words were not used in some situations, that would be a distortion of theology and the facts. The innumerable shades of neglect, deprivation, and oppression in this country do give us a more complex picture of our society than Gutiérrez has of his, and it also calls for a different political strategy. But our nation as such has direct responsibility for the condition which he rightly calls oppression.

One of the common criticisms of Gutiérrez is that he has reintroduced the utopian thinking that was the great error of the social gospel and is one great error of Marxism. He does use the word "utopia" favorably. He sees it as the "annunciation of what is not yet, but will be."[38] He speaks of "a new kind of man" and that does make me suspicious. However, it may be a shorthand way of saying that we need more than new structures; we need also new persons. New structures may educate people away from the predatory and callous egoism that is encouraged by the old structures. China seems to have been able to change the direction of the personal striving of her people. My question is the familiar question of Christian realism, the question as to how soon new forms of egoism will appear which will distort the new structures. Gutiérrez does not at this stage concern himself about the distortions of the new when people are being destroyed on a large scale by the distortions of the old. He does not deal much with the nature of the new structures or with the precise political strategies that are most viable in the various Latin-American countries. He does often speak of socialism in connection with the new structures. He speaks of "a new social consciousness" and "a social appropriation not only of the means of production, but also of the political process, and, definitively, of freedom."[39] I have said that his is a strategic theology for the present prerevolutionary situation. His projections for the future are hopeful and vague.

Gutiérrez knows enough about Christian teaching about sin and about the problematic character of human existence to set up important warning signals. He wants no "Christian ideology of political action or a politico-religious messianism." He sees the future promised by God as a gift and not a human work. He asks that we be kept "from any confusion of the Kingdom with any one historical stage, from any idolatry toward unavoidably ambiguous human achievement, from any absolutizing of revolution."[40] There are utopian tones in his theology, and this may be an inevitable consequence of having to live by hope in the midst of struggles that are today deeply frustrating. But he has not lost the understanding that comes to us both from Christian theology and from our universal experience that human achievements are "unavoidably ambiguous."

VI
A Return
to Economic Ethics

The theology of liberation that has its origin in Latin America should be a great stimulus to us in the United States. It has special importance as an address to citizens of this country on the use of their power in Latin America. It has little guidance for us so far as our own social and political agenda within the United States is concerned.

Possibilities for radical change by means of the political process still remain in this country. I do not want to generalize about possibilities in Latin America, but change there has come most often, if not by revolutions, at least by military coups. Those who hope and pray for revolutions from the left, as in Cuba, may be justified in their views concerning what would be best for their countries. At present the outlook for successful revolution of that sort is dim. My chief concern is that the United States abandon its counterrevolutionary policy in Latin America and elsewhere. The attempt to strangle the revolution in Cuba was as wrong as it has proved to be futile. The intervention in Chile through the C.I.A. to undercut the Allende regime is another example of what we should not do. The training of military officers, police, and antiguerrilla forces by the United States in order to keep in power oppressive regimes that are favorable to American economic interests or that win favor with us by being anti-Marxist makes us the guardians of a cruelly unjust *status quo* in that part of the world.

Whatever may be said about other countries, the most should be made here of the opportunities that remain for peaceful change. It is still possible to organize political movements either within our major political parties or as independent organizations to bring pressure on them. The freedom for dissent that exists here was illustrated by the extraordinary growth of sentiment against the war in Indochina. It was powerful enough to induce a president to retire. Courts and Congress on another set of issues forced another president to resign, and he was supplanted by as orderly a procedure for succession as has been known anywhere. The frustrations that have accompanied these events are natural, but they should not hide the fact that the political processes are still there to be used and that there is great freedom to organize to use them. I do not believe that there is as yet an adequate vision or a credible agenda among any of the groups that are contending for political power, but the widespread tendency to despair of politics is certainly premature.

It will sound bland to some readers to call attention to gains that have been made in recent decades, but not to do so would be to ignore an essential part of the picture. Here is one example. I remember the steel strike in 1919. It was one of the occasions on which representatives of the churches, at the cost of great controversy within the churches, made a real dent on public opinion. One of the issues in that strike was the right of the workers to organize into independent unions. The issue that received most publicity was the 12-hour day and, for many workers, the 7-day week. It is difficult to realize that within this century there were such conditions of wage slavery in the United States. In that period the industrial workers were at the mercy of their employers. Many corporations were little fascist states with their private armies of goons. The labor movement continued to struggle against great odds, with the state and the police generally on the side of employers, until the Wagner Act in 1935, which was an essential part of the New Deal legislation.

The conditions of unconscionable oppression and exploitation of industrial workers that were common before labor organizations gained strength are now largely forgotten. Today organized labor is relatively conservative. The blacks who are now struggling for equal opportunity to get jobs need help. Farm workers now need to share the advantages won by the industrial workers, and in this they are being aided by the AFL-CIO. I have deeply regretted the hawkishness of George Meany and many other labor leaders in regard to the Indochina war. This stems partly from their struggle with Communists in their unions in the 1930's and from a long-held view of foreign policy dominated by an absolutistic anti-Communism. New movements of neglected and oppressed people and new ideas are necessary, but it is a mistake to ignore the remarkable gains for a large segment of the American people that have been achieved by organized labor through its use of both economic and political power.

WEAKNESSES OF CAPITALISM

In preparing for what I want most to say I shall make some use of autobiography. In many ways I am a product of the great depression of the 1930's. The unemployment of 12,000,000 people, or about 25 percent of the labor force, was the most traumatic experience of Americans during that period. The New Deal, though distrusted by many as a means of propping up a decaying capitalism, proved to be a fresh start in American life. It gave hope of an indefinite continuation along the same lines of peaceful social change. However, during that period I was a committed socialist. I was a member of the Fellowship of Socialist Christians, of which Reinhold Niebuhr was the leader and prophet. Paul Tillich found it to be the nearest approach to the "religious socialism" of which he had been a major prophet in Germany. During that period I seldom made a speech or preached a sermon in which I did not have a section that was devoted to the structural injustice and the self-defeating nature of capitalism. I never had any interest in Communism as a movement in this country. For me democratic socialism, inspired in part by the socialistic tendencies that I found in Christianity, was the goal.

The theologians who influenced me most at the time were either avowed socialists or strong anticapitalists. This was true of the Reinhold Niebuhr of that period and of Paul Tillich. It was also true of Archbishop William Temple, who was a great inspiration to me both in theology and in social ethics. It was also true of the Emil Brunner of that period, the period in which he wrote *The Divine Imperative,* one of the most important books on social ethics of this century. Later he became more conservative, partly because of his fear of Communism, but his chapters on economic ethics are dominated by a radical anticapitalism. For example, Brunner says:

> It is that system in which all that we can see to be the meaning of the economic order from the point of view of faith is denied; in which, therefore, it is made impossible for the individual to realize, in any way, through his economic activity, the service of God and of his neighbor. This system is contrary to the spirit of service; it is debased and irresponsible; indeed, we may go further and say: it is irresponsibility developed into a system.[1]

I was not much influenced by Karl Barth at that time, but I knew that he had never abandoned his early socialism and that his anticapitalism became pronounced during the period of the cold war.

In 1937 the Oxford Conference on Church, Community, and State was convened, and by good fortune I had a role in preparation for it and was secretary of the section that dealt with the economic order. That conference was one of the great public events in my life. It also was one of the most significant events in the development of corporate thinking concerning social ethics in the ecumenical community. It was limited by the fact that it was chiefly Western in composition. Also it was held long before the development of close relations between Protestants and Catholics made possible by Vatican II. But in spite of these limitations it produced a body of corporate thought on social ethics that remains impressive and to which I go back for guidance on many issues. The section on economic issues with which I worked did not take a stand in favor of either a consistent socialism or a consistent capitalism. But it was profoundly critical of what it called "the economic order of the industrialized world." The paragraphs in its report that dealt with four criticisms of that economic order reflected the anticapitalism to which the theologians of that period were committed. I shall only give the main headings and follow them with a few key sentences. The four criticisms were that this economic order tended to enhance acquisitiveness, that it produced inequalities on a scale that challenged the Christian conscience, that it resulted in "irresponsible possession of economic power," and that it frustrated "the sense of Christian vocation." Consider also the following sentences:

> As long as industry is organized primarily not for the service of the community but with the object of producing a purely financial result for some of its members it cannot be recognized as properly fulfilling its social purpose.
>
> Any social arrangement which outrages the dignity of man by treating some men as ends and others as means, any institution which obscures the common humanity of men by emphasizing the external accidents of birth or wealth or social position, is *ipso facto* anti-Christian.
>
> It is still the case, even in some of the wealthy nations of western Europe, that large numbers of children undergo grave injury to their health before they reach the age of school attendance. . . .

Following the last sentence there was an idea expressed that today is more widely recognized to be of the gravest impor-

tance: "It often happens that these disadvantages are greatly
increased where economic opportunities are denied on racial grounds." The power wielded by a few individuals or
groups "gives the economic order in many countries some
resemblance to a tyranny."

Finally, one other form of work which seems clearly to
be in conflict with the Christian's vocation is the sales-
manship of a kind which involves deception—the deception which may be no more than insinuation and exaggeration, but which is a serious threat to the integrity of
the worker.

There under the heading of Christian vocation is a reference
to unemployment, the worst feature of which is seen to be
"the lack of significant activity which tends to destroy his (the
unemployed person's) self-respect." Also, this Oxford report
contains a very brief but extremely comprehensive and balanced discussion of the ethics of property. It emphasizes the
relative and contingent character of all human property
rights in the light of the belief in "God as the giver of all
wealth and as the creator of man's capacities to develop the
resources of nature." It also affirms that

the existing system of property rights and the existing
distribution of property must be criticized in the light of
the largely nonmoral processes by which they have been
developed, and criticism must take account of the fact
that every argument in defense of property rights which
is valid for Christian thinking is also an argument for the
widest possible distribution of these rights.

The report emphasized the importance of distinguishing between various forms of property, especially between property for personal use "which has clearer moral justification
than property in the means of production and in land which
gives owners power over other persons." Special concern is
expressed over the difficulty of bringing this kind of power
under adequate social control.[2]

Roman Catholic social teachings never fully accepted capitalism. There are sensible arguments for private property in the teachings of Thomas Aquinas, but they presuppose great limitations on property rights. Indeed the Catholic teaching is highly subversive of capitalistic assumptions concerning the rights of property. Thomas Aquinas says that "whatever certain people have in superabundance is due, by natural law, to the purpose of succouring the poor." He even goes so far as to say that under conditions of great urgency "it is lawful for a man to succour his own need by means of another's property, by taking it openly or secretly: nor is this properly speaking theft or robbery." He quotes a famous passage from St. Ambrose: "It is the hungry man's bread that you withhold, the naked man's cloak that you store away; the money that you bury in the earth is the price of the poor man's ransom and freedom."[3]

There is much the same spirit in Pope Paul's encyclical *Populorum Progressio,* from which I have quoted. The pope quotes a similar statement from Ambrose. The radical imperative that I have emphasized is deeply embedded in Christian social teaching, and in the light of this fact, whatever may be said concerning which type of economic system is in particular situations the greater good or the lesser evil, there must necessarily be deep tensions between churches and capitalism, which exaggerates self-interest and tends to create aggregates of private power that are difficult for agencies representing the public interest to keep accountable or responsible.

Eleven years later, in 1948 in Amsterdam, the First Assembly of the World Council of Churches addressed itself to the criticism of capitalism, and this time the word "capitalism" was used. What was said about capitalism balanced to some extent the criticisms that were made of what was called "the atheistic Marxian communism of our day." Again it was my privilege to have a part in this experience of ecumenical corporate thinking. I served as secretary of the Assembly's section on "The Church and the Disorder of Society." The criticisms of capitalism made by this report of the Assembly overlapped considerably with those made by the Oxford Conference. They were as follows:

> (1) Capitalism tends to subordinate what should be the primary task of any economy—the meeting of human needs—to the economic advantages of those who have most power over its institutions. (2) It tends to produce serious inequalities. (3) It has developed a practical form of materialism in western nations in spite of their Christian background for it has placed the greatest emphasis upon success in making money. (4) It has kept the people of capitalist countries subject to a kind of fate which has taken the form of such social catastrophes as mass unemployment.

It may be that capitalism now has developed protections against the degree of mass unemployment that was the catastrophe of the 1930's, but the other criticisms surely apply to capitalism as we know it in the United States. I have long been wary of speaking of systems and realize that the system of capitalism or free enterprise, which gives major emphasis to the private sector, has been modified in many ways in countries that may still be classified as capitalistic, including the United States. The American individualistic ethos or ideology, however, has created greater resistance to such modification than is present in many other Western nations such as the Scandinavian countries, Great Britain, and West Germany. We have since the New Deal—perhaps one may even say since the establishment of the progressive income tax—done many things to make the system more tolerable. But my purpose in writing this chapter is to suggest that a new leap forward is necessary. I shall come to that later.

After the 1930's two tendencies diverted me from my interest in socialism. One was the Second World War and the preoccupation with the many political problems that it raised, such as the whole question of the justification of mili-

tary action against Hitler's Germany and the preparation for
the political policies and institutions that would be important
for the peace. The other was that I became confident that the
New Deal had made possible a more humane and just form
of capitalism. I emphasized the importance of avoiding ideological debates about systems and of accepting the idea of a
mixed economy on a somewhat pragmatic basis. However,
for me pragmatism was never without a sense of direction
involving standards of justice under the pull of the idea of
equality. The checklist of the moral weaknesses of capitalism
was never far from my mind. Always I emphasized the conviction that public economic initiative had no less a moral
claim than private economic initiative and that often it had
a surer claim. The idea (which I still find prevalent in the
United States) that what is done by private agencies is somehow inherently better than what is done by public agencies,
is, I think, the error that causes us to be less effective than we
might be when we cannot escape public forms of economic
initiative and control.

Contra
Reaganomics

In the early 1950's I participated in an ambitious study of
economic ethics sponsored by the National Council of
Churches and financed without any strings by the Rockefeller Foundation. As an example of the collaboration of theologians and social scientists, mostly economists, this study was
significant. As I look back upon it in the context of that period
it seems to me now to have been bland, an expression of the
confidence in American affluence that was so general at the
time. The study was based on the assumption that the pie
would continually get larger and that poverty would be overcome by giving everyone a larger slice. What a contrast to
our experience today and also to the growing recognition
that resources are finite and that, while growth in the so-
called developing countries must continue, American economic growth will and should be limited. My own contributions to the study were probably to the left, if one must use
that word as shorthand, of most of the others. I greatly re-

spected the moral sensitivity of the economists and I can testify that, whatever methods they may have used in other segments of their discipline, in this study their thinking was not "value free." This was as true of those who, as economists, gave priority to freedom as it was of those who gave priority to justice. Most of them could not be classified so neatly. I learned from them better than I would have been able to learn from fellow theologians or students of ethics what unexpected problematic by-products may result from the best-intentioned policies. That is one thing on which economists seem to be experts.

I lived in the rather optimistic world of the mixed economy that seemed slowly to be becoming more just and humane for nearly two more decades, during which time other issues diverted my attention from economic ethics. I was diverted by issues of race that at the time had more to do with law and social relations than with economics, though today the economic plight of minority groups is perhaps the most stubborn aspect of racial injustice. I was diverted by the foreign policy issues of the cold war and especially of the war in Indochina. I still believe that ideological conflicts and sometimes fear for national security, whether justified or not, have had a larger part in both than have American economic interests, private or public. But I realize that this is now a matter of furious debate. Today I believe that I need to return to economic issues as having central importance for Christian ethics. In what follows I shall not attempt to do more than suggest an agenda. I hope that those who with me have neglected economic ethics will give fresh attention to American economic institutions and policies.

NEEDED ECONOMIC CHANGES

I shall distinguish between several changes that can be made in our economic institutions along the lines that have already been followed since the New Deal, and changes that involve raising much deeper questions than are commonly raised about the free enterprise system itself. I realize that this distinction is not one that can be made in absolute terms. There is a gray area where those changes which may be regarded as "reforms" imply some modification of the deeper assumptions about priorities in the system.

I shall give as examples four reforms that are possible now or in the near future. They are already a part of current political debates and there is widespread public readiness for them. In practice they will come by means of legislative compromise and there will always be the question as to whether the heart of the reform has been compromised away. My interest here is not to deal with the details of various compromises, and I do not claim competence to do so, but rather it is to put these four reforms together in the minds of readers in order to indicate that much can still be done now without waiting for answers to the deeper questions that must be raised.

The first of these reforms is a system to make medical care available to the whole population without bankrupting anyone. The present situation cries to heaven and most Americans know this, not least those in the middle classes whose medical bills often bring them close to bankruptcy. Medicare for persons over sixty-five was ideologically a significant breakthrough. Organized medicine, by its resistance to this program and to all movements away from professional individualism, has lost credibility. Now fortunately there is a significant split within the profession on issues of publicly sponsored medical insurance for the whole population.

The second reform is the establishment of a system of income maintenance which would guarantee to all persons a minimum income that would come to be taken for granted as their right as much as it is now taken for granted that they have the right to send their children to free public schools. President Nixon, prodded by Daniel Moynihan, did present a plan that might have been an important entering wedge for a more adequate program. This was defeated by a coalition of conservatives who rejected the basic principle and liberals who thought that the ceiling for the guaranteed income was too low and who feared that the "workfare" element that was built into it might become a system of forced labor. Milton Friedman, known for his conservative individualism as an economist, has proposed a negative income tax, which would be one way of guaranteeing such a minimum income. Dissatisfaction with the humiliating aspects of the welfare system, its failure to provide a minimum income for the working poor, and the unjust differences in its provisions from state to state has prepared the ground for acceptance of this reform. It would make an enormous difference to the lives of the poorest sixth of our people.

3. The third reform is changes in the tax system that would close loopholes for the rich and in many ways bring about a more equal distribution of wealth. The adoption of the idea of a progressive income tax was in itself an early breakthrough of great importance. But there is endless ingenuity in rigging taxes so that they favor those who have the most economic power in the nation. Some states refuse to have income taxes. The sales tax is politically the easiest to impose, but it is regressive. The social security tax is regressive because it is taken on about the first fourteen thousand dollars of income. The use of the tax system as an incentive to corporations to encourage needed investment or needed innovations may be justified so long as it is fully publicized and continually reviewed. Taxes illustrate an area in which human sinfulness is easily spotted, because people almost always try to have the chief burden of taxation fall on other groups than their own. All persons are experts on how taxes affect their own groups. The moral issue takes on the most serious proportions when the injustice of the tax structure is disguised or when particular groups are able to bring undue influence on the members of Congress who make the decisions about taxes. Campaign contributions are one form of

"honest" influence that is now under greater criticism than ever before, but belonging to the same crowd gives rise to a natural form of influence that will continue to operate.

The fourth reform is to carry out consistently the implications of the idea of the Government as the employer of last resort. I have emphasized earlier the scandal of the high percentage of unemployed young persons in our cities, especially among minorities, and of the failure of our nation and its Government to deal directly with this socially disastrous situation. Official national unemployment statistics, though they have already reached almost 9 percent unemployed in the recession of 1974-1975, do not reveal fully the gravity of the situation. They need to be broken down by regions and cities. Also, they fail to include those who have despaired of finding work and have ceased to apply for it.

These four familiar reforms taken together would go far to make American economic institutions more just and humane. Yet I believe that we need to go beyond them and take more seriously two structural flaws in the free enterprise system itself. The first is the neglect of social needs that private enterprise cannot meet and also make profits. The second is the existence of vast private economic empires whose power is only slightly tamed by the community.

There are, to be sure, many public needs that private enterprise does not and cannot meet. This is readily accepted in the case of education. It has been accepted in the case of systems of highways because they are so necessary for private enterprise. Any public enterprise connected with national defense fits the pattern of public initiative that is gladly accepted. There are many examples of the initiative of government in providing for low-cost housing and for public transportation. But in these cases inhibitions that stem from the doctrine of individualism and from the assumption that private enterprise is inherently better than public enterprise cripple the community's public efforts to meet its own needs. Could there be a clearer case of this than our experience of public transportation? The railroads are allowed to decay and eventually may have to be taken over by agencies of the community under the worst possible conditions. The desperate need for public transportation that enables people to get to their work is extremely difficult to meet, partly because of the resistance of the powerful vested interests in private transportation, and partly because public economic initiative on a large scale goes against the grain. Years ago the social consequences of these individualistic inhibitions were vividly expressed by John Kenneth Galbraith when he contrasted our private wealth with our public poverty. Prevailing assumptions about the American way of life make it difficult to realize how much public poverty robs people of private well-being. My concern at this point is to work for the overcoming of the ideological inhibitions that prevent the community at all levels from adventurously inventing new agencies responsible to itself for meeting its own neglected needs.

More difficult and also more fundamental is the taming of private economic empires. Monopolistic or semimonopolistic private economic power is not adequately tamed by the accepted forms of public regulation, for it often has too much influence over the regulators. The influence exercised on Congress and on the administration through campaign contributions has been more fully exposed than ever before by the events associated with Watergate. The socialist argument in favor of nationalizing economic enterprises that become too powerful to be effectively regulated would seem to be quite persuasive in principle. The immediate need is to develop models for public control, but here again ideological inhibitions prevent us from making the effort to develop models that may be effective and responsible to the public.

There is a passage in an encyclical of Pope Pius XI, *Quadragesimo Anno*, published in 1931, that gives the basic ethical principle to which I am appealing. After referring to some changes in the ideas of socialists, he said:

If these changes continue it may well come about that gradually the tenets of mitigated socialism will no longer be different from the program of those who seek to reform human society according to Christian principles. For it is rightly contended that certain forms of property must be reserved to the state, since they carry with them an opportunity of domination too great to be left to private individuals without injury to the community at large. (Par. 114)

Those papal words may seem too cautious to many readers. However, in 1931 the deep Roman Catholic antipathy toward socialism made that quite an adventurous statement. Today it would be necessary to add the phrase "structures of management" to the reference to property. Also, the state may best be only the agent of the community that enables the community to create forms of control that have some independence of the state. What the pope said is in line with the corporate teachings of the ecumenical movement that is now embodied in the World Council of Churches, on which I have also drawn.

I am not returning to a belief that I held in the 1930's— a belief in a comprehensive system of socialism as a panacea, or almost a panacea. The total union of economic and political power could well be more oppressive than some degree of pluralism among private economic empires that coexist with a democratic state. My reason for writing this chapter is to urge a new generation of persons concerned about Christian ethics to press the socialistic questions even though they do not accept ready-made socialistic answers. A new debate is needed about economic institutions, and on a much more fundamental level. Those of us who spent ten years resisting the state in connection with the war in Vietnam should not now choose economic institutions that have as their chief characteristic the extension of the power of the state. A public bureaucracy such as the Defense Department develops its own vested interests, which need to be opposed by a free press—and the press is not likely to be free from governmental intimidation without a private sector that can support it. Christian teaching about the depth and pervasiveness of self-interest is a warning against uncritical confidence in any pattern of institutions or in any "system." There is no Christian system, but there are motives, criteria, goals, and forms of self-criticism inspired by their faith by which Christians should test all institutions and systems. The freedom of the church from the state may have its greatest importance in the next period. The church is free to be a conscience within the nation that is responsive to universal human needs and that will be a check on the kind of militarism that distorts American economic life.

There is a need for pluralism in government that goes beyond the constitutional checks and balances. It must be embodied in forms of public initiative and administration in economic life that are independent of the regular rhythms of politics. Perhaps the system of independent courts is an analogy that has some value. Various methods of choosing members of governing boards are needed that diversify the constituencies represented and spread the power of choice.

What we now call a "mixed economy" is not pluralistic enough because it allows enormous aggregates of private economic power from private economic motives and with the use of great private resources to thwart the efforts of public bodies to regulate them.

The word "private" will seem out of date to those who stress that there is a new breed of managers and technicians who are professionals and quite different from the individualistic entrepreneurs of an earlier period. I am using the word "private" to refer to institutions that are not subject to controls that put the broadest public interest above more limited interests. Insofar as the representatives of this new breed do have professional motives or a professional ethos they would be released to be more fully themselves if the institutions that they serve were held to account for the sake of the broader public interest. Such persons can be expected to have some openness to new patterns, and they should have an important part in the next stage of the debate. Debate and experiment, experiment and debate on many levels without the blinders of the individualistic ideology that is still so pervasive are what is needed now while the compensatory reforms that I have emphasized earlier in this chapter are pursued. Sometimes this approach, which is not controlled by confidence in a comprehensive future pattern, is dismissed as an example of pragmatism. There is a pragmatic element in it but it is a pragmatism that has a definite sense of direction, that sees how to apply clear ethical criteria to past and present institutions and policies, and that is always aware of ethical limits. Some skepticism about future patterns and some humility about prescribing solutions seem to me to be very much in order.

FATEFUL INFLATION

I shall now attempt to approach economic ethics by another route. I am led to do this because of the fateful importance of inflation as a sickness of the economic order that can defeat most of our ethical purposes. As I have said, I am in some ways a product of the depression of the 1930's and as such I have to shift gears in thinking about the threat of inflation. Also, I strongly suspect that neither socialists nor the advocates of free enterprise in the economy have very sure answers to the problem of inflation. A socialist country that is at all dependent on foreign trade certainly has no solution for itself alone. Whether a self-contained socialism might be inflation-proof or merely better able to disguise inflation I do not know.

Inflation is a highly technical problem. The technical experts are not in agreement about how to deal with it. If the experts on problems involving both ethics and technical expertise agreed on either diagnosis or cure, the task of those who have primarily ethical concerns would be much simpler, but this is seldom the case. This is true in part because technical experts are conditioned by the interests of the social groups to which they belong and by the frames of reference, the priorities, the ideologies that develop in the circles in which they move. Whatever the reasons, this is a profound problem of the psychology and sociology of knowledge. In practice much more is required than piling data upon data or expert judgments upon expert judgments.

Obviously there is no Christian or, even in a broad sense, ethical solution or series of solutions in this area. However, there are issues in the discussion of inflation in which those concerned about ethics have a great stake. In what follows I shall deal with five ethical issues involved in the decisions that are made about inflation.

The first ethical issue is the effect of inflation, or the effect of the measures that are taken to counteract it, on the people who are most vulnerable and most likely to suffer. Politicians talk about equity in the bearing of the burdens imposed by inflation but, as I write, little more than lip service has been given to it by those who have most power to make decisions. Some policies are projected to help the unemployed when the rate of unemployment rises to a particular percentage, but this takes little account of those already unemployed. Little is projected to help the elderly who are on low fixed incomes and the poor in general, who spend a larger proportion of their incomes than the more privileged spend on food, the cost of which rises more rapidly than that of most commodities. The amount of silent suffering on the part of people who are not well organized to protest and who have little political power as a group is very great now, and there is no sign that it will diminish. I need not enlarge on this ethical issue, the effect of inflation on those who are most vulnerable, because much of this book has stressed the claims of the most oppressed people, but it is clearly the place to begin as we discuss the subject of inflation.

The second ethical issue has to do with participation in the process of decision-making of all groups most affected by inflation or by policies designed to combat it. This is true of all important economic problems, but the technical nature of inflation creates a danger that it may be left to a limited group of experts. There was some value in the large and rather representative conference on economics called by President Gerald Ford in October 1974. It did expose the public as a whole to the broad social problems that were involved. The conference may have caused the administration to take more seriously than it was inclined to do the fact that the country was suffering from a recession as well as from inflation and the probability that the methods used to combat inflation would tend to aggravate the recession and result in a serious increase in unemployment. The labor leaders who were present were able to make their case quite powerfully on this point to the public and to the administration. This was an example of participation by many of the people most affected, but there was no adequate participation by those who represented the elderly or other less articulate segments of the poor, who are always the last to be heard.

A third ethical issue has to do with the decisions about where the deepest cuts should be made in the budget. One major question is raised by debates about the defense budget. Should that be cut in order to avoid having to cut items that are important for the welfare of people in other parts of the budget? There is a tendency to treat the defense budget as especially privileged and to protect it against its share of cuts. Those who are pacifists on principle may come to the quick conclusion that most military expenditures can be cut, because the whole military establishment is without justification. However, even many pacifists would admit that a government responsible to a nation that is not made up of pacifists cannot adopt such a policy. I find myself in the difficult position of deeply distrusting the military arm of government and yet of admitting that in an armed world unilateral disarmament would be both politically nonviable and wrong. Unilateral initiatives in disarmament should be tried, for an endless arms race is a great risk for all humanity. In thinking about the defense budget, there should be guidance from persons who are experts on the real strength of the United States relative to that of other powers, but who are not themselves influenced by the vested interests of the Defense Department. We need from them objective judgments concerning the meaning of *sufficiency* at a time when both great nuclear powers have the capacity for overkill. Parts of our civilian government, including the armed services committees of Congress and sometimes also the president, tend to be in awe of the military. They do not take sufficiently into account the occupational insatiability of military leadership influenced by its industrial suppliers. Thinking about military sufficiency is often controlled by ideas of American global domination that are foolish and wrong; by ideas of the cold war that read unlimited intentions of expansion into Russian actions and that are out of date; and by a failure to realize that the years and years of bellicose anti-Communism on the part of our leaders has made our nation an object of fear in Communist countries. When we try to measure the degree to which either the capacity or the intentions of nations are to be feared it is well to remember that the United States is the only nation that has ever used nuclear bombs, and that it has employed more military force since the Second World War than all the other nations of the world put together. Taking all these considerations into account would probably cause those who make decisions to be ready to make sizable reductions in the defense budget for the benefit of all.

A fourth ethical issue involved in inflation is the scale of values that should govern consumption of economic goods. People are told to consume less. They also are told that as a nation Americans consume 40 percent of the world's resources though they make up only 6 percent of the world's people. It is estimated that one American draws upon resources that would sustain, on a mere subsistence level, fifty persons in India.[4] The pressures of inflation make this a good time to reconsider the ethics of our economy, which usually encourages constantly increasing consumption.

One of the criticisms of capitalism that was much emphasized in ecumenical circles in the 1930's and 1940's is that there is a fundamental irrationality in capitalistic institutions. To a considerable extent consumption is for the sake of production, rather than production being for the sake of consumption. How else can we explain the great emphasis on obsolescence? How else can we explain the dynamics of that large part of the advertising business which attempts to persuade people to want new things that they surely do not need? When we think of the world's limited resources and the need of scaling down American consumption of them these tendencies that are built into our economy are as unjust in a global context as they are irrational. How many people on other continents must die to preserve this absurd pattern of consumption in prosperous northern countries, and not least in our own?

This leads me to the fifth moral issue related to inflation, perhaps the hardest one of all to face squarely. How far are we going to keep our food to ourselves because the cost of food is rising so fast in this country? How far will we be willing—politically willing—to export food to countries that are already in the grip of famine, threatened by famine, or in which hundreds of millions of people are badly undernourished? The figures used by those in a position to know the grim facts are to me incredible as I try to imagine what they mean in human terms. John Knowles, president of the Rockefeller Foundation, said in March 1974 that "among the two and a half billion people living in the world's less developed countries, 60% are estimated to be malnourished . . . and 20% are believed to be starving at this moment."[5] Robert S. McNamara, as president of the World Bank, in October 1974 released similar statistics. A major article in *The Wall Street Journal* on October 3, 1974, said: "To most Americans hunger is an occasional pang of a delayed meal or a skipped breakfast. But for an estimated seven hundred million people, hunger is commonplace and the prospect of an agonizing death by starvation a grim fact of life. . . . Half of them are children." Five days later the same journal carried this headline: "U.S. Response to Hunger Elsewhere Is Likely to Be Modest."

The question to be faced is twofold: Will we make more than a token contribution to the desperate need for food in other parts of the world and will we do this without causing the poorest people in this country to do most of the sacrificing? The human emergency is so immense and so tragic that no well-fed country with great resources can adhere to a pattern of business as usual. There is no question about the facts. Churches have a responsibility to take initiative not only by organizing their own distribution of food but also by thinking through what the nation can do politically. This is an area of such clear obligation that there must be a very broad public conscience to which appeal can be made.

All the usual ideas about doing only what can be seen as serving the national interest are insufficient. In April 1963, Walter Lippmann, who on foreign policy issues did greatly stress the national interest, published a column in which he said: "The poor wretches who have to sell foreign aid to Congress have been taught that they are advocates of an act of unnatural generosity. The cardinal rule is that they must avoid the suspicion that our motives in giving foreign aid are in the smallest degree disinterested. . . . The accepted way to get the money voted is for the President to cross his heart and swear that every dollar will be used to hire allies and to confound our adversaries." Later in the same column Lippmann said: "It is a duty, not merely in the national interest, of all nations, rich and poor alike, to provide the funds to finance world development." How much more so when the purpose is to fight famine. Senator J. W. Fulbright in 1965 wrote: "It is difficult to see how the rich countries can expect to be secure in their affluence as islands in a global sea of misery. But beyond the social and economic and political and strategic reasons for the rich aiding the poor is the simple motive of humanitarian conscience."[6] This kind of thinking is needed on the level of statesmanship. It is important to avoid using language or symbols that suggest that the United States even expects gratitude. It is possible to stretch the idea of national interest so that in a real sense it is seen to be against the national interest for the citizens of our country, if they have consciences at all, to live in the presence of starving people. An appeal not to generosity that expects gratitude but to an elemental feeling for humanity would get more support in Congress and among the people than appeals to some expected political benefit in international relations. It is true that there is a psychological difficulty when people feel that they have been made poorer by inflation, but even this could become a way of beginning to have a sense of solidarity with other peoples. To recognize the precariousness rather than the pride of riches may be a good point to begin to have new thoughts concerning the place of our country in the world.

I am still enough of a Christian realist to be inhibited about expecting profound changes of attitude in a nation as a whole, because there is a stubborn self-centeredness that easily gets moral support from ideas of national interest which in other contexts may be legitimate. But today the issues that we face are so grave, the simplest requirements of human concern for others are so clear, that a deep change in what people feel to be important to them and a real conversion of the mind and heart is called for. What is at stake overshadows the issues of the cold war that used to seem so important. Two things are at stake: the survival of a large part of humanity, and the humanity of those who survive because they live in privileged and protected countries.

VII
What Should Be Learned from the Indochina War

On May 7, 1970, on the invitation of the Foreign Relations Committee of the United States Senate, I gave testimony to my strongly held belief that our country was engaged in an unjust war in Indochina. Others who testified with me were Roman Catholic Bishop John J. Dougherty and Rabbi Irving Greenberg. We were invited as individuals by the committee and not chosen as representatives by our religious communities. The members of the committee took the testimony seriously and spent three hours on the subject. The fact that such testimony was invited by an important agency of government at a time when a costly and destructive war was being waged is itself of some significance. I used the phrase "unjust war" in order to relate what I said to the traditional Christian thinking on the subject. I believe that the experience of the Indochina war may prove to be a watershed in the life of the church, since in such a decisive way the contrast between just and unjust wars was used to proclaim that a particular war was unjust. Most often this distinction has been used to justify particular wars in which one's own nation was engaged. The first part of my testimony was as follows:

As background it may be helpful to raise the question as to the point at which the war itself becomes a matter of morality. When do we move beyond the judgment that it is a mistake of giant proportions to the judgment that it is an immoral war? In what I say I am not passing judgment on the personal motives of the various leaders who have initiated or escalated our involvement in Vietnam. However, good intentions based upon illusions can create an objective situation of moral horror and one that leads innumerable individuals into callous or brutal conduct and undermines the moral fiber of a nation and its institutions.

I do not see how we can draw an absolute line between an intellectual mistake and moral failure, because when the nation and its leaders persist in the mistake for years, after its consequences for people in this country and in Vietnam are fully revealed, and when it becomes patent that this persistence in destructive error is a concession to the pride of a nation that has never been defeated, it is time to see even the mistake in a context that calls for moral judgments.

The traditional thinking about the difference between a just and an unjust war in the churches has always placed great emphasis on two considerations and I believe that both of these are relevant to the discussion of this war. The first is really a commonsense view of the degree to which the injury done to societies by the war is out of proportion to the good that can be achieved. One criterion of the just war, which may seem on the surface to suggest a rather craven caution, is that there should be a reasonable chance of success. But seen in the light of the principle of proportionality, this means that a nation should not sacrifice its sons or slaughter the people on the other side or ravage their country when the purpose for doing this cannot be realized. It seems to me that our leaders should have come to see that no amount of firepower from the air or from the land can create a nation in South Vietnam and establish a government around which that nation can rally.

The other emphasis in the discussion of the difference between a just and an unjust war has to do with the conduct of the war by means of policies and acts which are morally wrong in themselves, and here we should have in mind especially the treatment of civilians or helpless persons such as prisoners.

As we look at the record of what has happened in Vietnam, there are these two levels of immorality. One is the cumulative destruction of persons and communities and even nature itself by acts of war which might in individual cases be regarded as inevitable if there is to be a war at all. The body count, the destruction of towns and villages, the uprooting of people from their homes, turning them into refugees by the millions, the ecological damage which is now being seen to have long-term effects on the land—these over a period of six years add up to a terrible accumulation of disproportionate evil. This is an evil for both sides, but it has a new dimension when we see how the most powerful nation in the world has kept inflicting it on the helpless people of Vietnam, and now the people of Laos and Cambodia must be added. The United States seems to be a captive of the momentum of its own destructive power.

When we move from this cumulative evil to particular acts which in any circumstances are immoral in themselves it is even clearer what the fighting of the war has done to Americans. The recent revelation of the massacres at Song My makes vivid the nature of this war as no other single event has done, but it differs only in degree from many less publicized episodes involving the killing of noncombatants and the torture of prisoners either by our own people or by proxy by the South Vietnamese. One of the most significant developments in the discussion of Song My was the tendency of journalists to raise the question as to the difference between killing helpless people, including children, on the ground at short range when they are seen and the killing of them from the air, at longer range, when they are not seen in so-called "free-fire" zones. I realize that the psychological difference is very great, but how great is the moral difference when it is well known that there will often be many of the same helpless victims?

The most obvious effects of this war on the life of our country are that it has bitterly divided our people and that it has so diverted our attention and so used our national resources that we make no progress in solving national problems that cry to heaven for solution. The decay of our cities continues and tens of millions of our people remain victims of a culture of poverty and many of these of an oppressive racism. At home we seem to be a "pitiful helpless giant" while we try to prove to the world that we are not one by a compulsive aggressiveness.

I did not know in May 1970 to what an extent even important figures in the administration who had been architects of the American war policy or at least very close to decision-making had had serious moral questions about what they were doing as early as 1967.

Townsend Hoopes, who was Under Secretary of the Air Force under President Johnson, after he left office published a book entitled *The Limits of Intervention*, which tells at length about his own disillusionment concerning the American war policy, of which he was an important civilian representative. In one passage he tells about the feelings of one of his colleagues in the Pentagon, John T. McNaughton, and vividly brings out this moral questioning at the heart of government. McNaughton was Assistant Secretary of Defense (International Security Affairs) and, judging from the Pentagon Papers, he was one of the chief idea men in the Pentagon. He was a very close adviser of Secretary of Defense Robert S. McNamara. Hoopes relates the following episode:

McNaughton was by the spring of 1967 appalled by the catastrophic loss of proportion that had overtaken the U.S. Military effort in Vietnam. "We seem to be proceeding," he said to me in barbed tones, after returning from a particular White House session, "on the assumption that the way to eradicate the Viet Cong is to destroy all village structures, to defoliate all jungles, and then cover the entire surface of South Vietnam with asphalt."[1]

Even more remarkable is a statement by Secretary McNamara, who was not only a chief architect of the American policy in Indochina but also one who took it upon himself to try to persuade the American people, often in very optimistic terms, to support the policy. The Pentagon Papers reveal that he wrote a memorandum in May 1967 to President Johnson that contained the following words:

> The picture of the world's greatest super-power killing or seriously injuring 1,000 non-combatants a week while trying to pound a tiny backward nation into submission on an issue whose merits are hotly disputed is not a pretty one.[2]

Those words are an intentional understatement. There is a patronizing tone in the reference to the "tiny backward nation" that is related to the psychological distance between our people and the Vietnamese—a distance that made it easier to pound them so cruelly for so long—but the words give a hint of the moral conflict over the war that was felt in high places six years before the end of our country's major involvement. The pounding went on six years longer. It became more furious in the case of North Vietnam, and after 1970 Cambodia was also a target. Soon after sending that memorandum McNamara resigned as Secretary of Defense. His going to an international organization, the World Bank, may explain his failure publicly to follow up that statement.

Even as early as 1965 Assistant Secretary McNaughton had prepared a memorandum for the Pentagon to provide a general rationale for this country's involvement in Vietnam. To read his estimate of those reasons now is revealing, for they are in sharp contrast with presidential rhetoric at the time. The reason given 70 percent weight was, "To avoid a humiliating U.S. defeat" (which would destroy our reputation as a guarantor). The reason given 20 percent weight was, "To keep South Vietnam [and then adjacent territory] from Chinese hands." The reason given 10 percent weight was, "To permit the people of South Vietnam to enjoy a better, freer way of life." He added that one of the Government's goals was "to emerge from the crisis without unacceptable taint from methods used" and also that we were not there "to help a friend . . . , although it would be hard to stay in if asked out."[3]

I am not suggesting that this memorandum as early as 1965 was normative for all thinking in the Government, but it is revealing because of the influence of its author in the Pentagon. Early in the war there were probably many persons responsible for policy who sincerely believed that it was possible to achieve results favorable to the people of South Vietnam. As it became less likely that increased use of military force would create the conditions for a viable and somewhat free government in South Vietnam, the emphasis on avoiding an American defeat became more and more important. The spectacle of able and sometimes elegant men sitting in Washington deciding to keep bombing the whole of Indochina year after year, without regard to the consequences for people or for environment, in order to solve an American problem—the avoidance of an American defeat—is abhorrent. We get the full force of this only now that we can look back upon nearly ten years of war. Sometimes when such things are said it is suggested that they are moralistic and self-righteous. There is a danger that some warnings against moralism and self-righteousness may shield us from facing the depth of the wrongs for which we share responsibility.

How We Got Involved

I have begun with moral criticism of the way in which the war in Indochina was conducted by the United States. In order to learn from this terrible experience as a nation we need to know why our country became involved in such a combination of almost universally admitted errors and widely admitted wrongs. I shall not deal with the particular steps into the abyss but shall discuss two aspects of our Ameri-

can self-understanding and outlook on the world that under-
lay those steps.

The first is the American sense of a unique role and destiny, which goes back to the earliest settlements in New
England and which has been an essential part of the national
consciousness, though today it may be little more than
residual. The settlers in New England were seeking to found
an ideal commonwealth on a new continent without being
limited by all that was tragic and sinful in European experience. The new community was believed to be a new Israel
of God. Long after the original and often devout interpreters
of the new community had passed away we find such a sophisticated commentator as John Adams saying the following: "I always consider the settlement of America as the
opening of a grand design of Providence for the illumination
of the ignorant and the emancipation of the slavish part of
mankind all over the earth."[4] This attitude toward people
abroad is revealing, and the reference to "the slavish part of
mankind" is ironic since Adams' own generation caused slavery to become part of the law of the land in the new nation.

One of the finer statements of this sense of role and destiny
is found in Lincoln's way of putting it. He referred to the
American people as "the almost chosen people" and thereby
left room for the judgment upon them which he so elo-
quently expressed in his Second Inaugural. Lincoln also said
that this experiment in self-government was "the last, best
hope of earth." While that statement may have been exces-
sive, even today many non-Americans say something like
this: If the United States cannot make it, who can? If this
country should prove to be unable to realize greater justice
and at the same time preserve what is central in its constitutional grounding of personal freedom, there is little hope in
the long run for such a union of justice and freedom elsewhere.

The claims for the American role and destiny became
especially pretentious and strident near the end of the nine-

teenth century. As various historians have their favorite examples of wild things said about wealth and poverty, to which I have referred, so they have their favorite examples of this astonishing national hubris. There are three that are especially striking, two of them from the religious community. The most famous is by Senator Albert J. Beveridge of Indiana, one of the leaders of the Progressive movement and the biographer of John Marshall. After saying that "God has made the English speaking and Teutonic peoples the master organizers of the world to establish system where chaos reigns," he said that "of all our race he has marked the American people as his chosen nation to finally lead in the regeneration of the world."[5] In the religious community two influential Protestant leaders spoke in the same vein. Josiah Strong, a major representative of the social gospel, at one time a secretary of the Congregational Home Missionary Society, and a progressive churchman in his day, wrote as follows in 1885 in his very popular book, *Our Country:*

> It is manifest that the Anglo-Saxon holds in his hands the destinies of mankind and it is evident that the United States is to become the home of this race, the principal seat of his power, the great center of his influence. . . . Does it not look as if God were not only preparing in our Anglo-Saxon civilization the die with which to stamp the peoples of the earth, but as if he were also massing behind the die the mighty power with which to press it?[6]

As if that were not enough, more than a generation later a leading Methodist bishop, Warren A. Candler, declared: "The hope of mankind is in the keeping of the Anglo-Saxon nations, led by the United States; and evangelical Christianity, with Methodism in the forefront, is the hope of these nations."[7] None of those men were crackpots; they were much admired leaders in their time. It is one sign of progress that such statements could only be made by crackpots today.

Today persons comparable to these men in stature not only could not say such things; they could not think them. This kind of grandiose messianism is dead, though there does remain as a little acknowledged force a considerable remnant of the Anglo-Saxon and northern European racism.

Those feelings about America do have importance as background for attitudes that in recent years have been very powerful. I suggest that these attitudes contain at least two elements. One is the widely held assumption that there is an American solution to nearly every problem on earth and that if Americans try hard enough it may be realized. In Indochina we tried very hard using the instruments we understood, especially bombs, and we now know the results. The other common attitude that dominated policymakers when they were first becoming involved in Indochina, and that many of them have continued to hold with some reservations until now, was an absolutistic anti-Communism. Today this view most often takes the form of an insistence that Communism cannot be tolerated in this hemisphere, in Chile for example. There is a much less intransigent attitude toward Communism in China or the Soviet Union.

The old messianism that was so grandiose and exuberant is no longer strong among us, yet this optimism about American solutions and their relevance is only now slowly disappearing. Anti-Communism as a mark of the national mission, while losing force, is still with us. As recently as 1970 John K. Fairbank, the best known of American experts on the history of China, wrote that "today the greatest menace to mankind may well be the American tendency to over-respond to heathen evils abroad, either by attacking them or by condemning them to outer darkness."[8] He wrote before the surprising rapprochement with China initiated by President Richard Nixon. The favorable response among the American people to that development is a sign that, even when there are deep tendencies in the American consciousness of the kind Fairbank noted, there are other countervailing tendencies as well. Great changes can come rather quickly.

The American sense of mission at its best, as Abraham Lincoln expressed it, did not mean that our country should impose its will on other peoples by force. It was rather a matter of example, of demonstrating that the American experiment was workable, and that it could survive such a trial as the Civil War. I do not believe that even today this sense of mission should be renounced, but in terms of its recent manifestations it needs to be transformed. The establishment of a new nation with freedoms so strongly protected by a constitution, so different in its ideal of equality from most traditional societies, and with its radical ethnic pluralism, is no small thing. The test of it will be its capacity to achieve racial equality and new levels of economic justice. Also it should be accompanied by a reversal of the tendency to feel contempt toward the social experiments of other nations, by growth in humility, by restraint in the use of power abroad, and by a willingness to help relieve the distress of less favored peoples without seeking to control them. There is good reason to be proud that so great a movement of dissent was possible in time of war. The fact that our country's use of overwhelming force in Indochina failed to achieve its purposes may become an important factor in this needed transformation. The disproof of what D. W. Brogan long ago called "the illusion of American omnipotence" had to come. It came in a tragic way and at terrible cost to the people of Indochina and to our own people. The churches have both a prophetic and a pastoral responsibility to help their members understand the meaning of failure. A prophetic interpretation of meaning can be a source of pastoral support of morale. There is a large minority, especially among the younger generation, that is ready to understand.

Against this broad background of American self-confidence and sense of mission, there were some specific developments after the Second World War that help to explain our involvement in Indochina. One was the fact that the leaders of the United States had had great success in their intervention in Europe to defeat Hitler's Germany. They had also helped enormously in the rebuilding of Europe, including the lands of both allies and enemies. They readily came to believe that they could have the same success in solving the problems of Southeast Asia. They did not realize the difference between helping the European nations—with their traditions of self-government and their combination of industrial development and pressures for social justice—to become themselves again and attempting to create a new nation in South Vietnam, which had no recent experience of self-government and which remained in a revolutionary situation. To intervene in a double revolutionary civil war both within South Vietnam and between North and South Vietnam was to enter an abyss. No amount of firepower could have achieved American purposes. The major who said that he had destroyed a village in order to save it gave us a paradigm for the whole operation in Indochina. We may thank God that in desperation our Government did not use nuclear bombs in Indochina. Was this the result of wise restraint or moral inhibitions? Or was it the result of awareness that the Soviet Union also had nuclear bombs? Probably both.

Throughout the personal struggles with motives and the public debates connected with the Indochina war there was great emphasis on the American responsibility to contain Communism. The decisions that set the stage for involvement in war came in the early years of the cold war when during the Truman administration our Government chose to support French colonialism in Indochina. This was done in part to secure French cooperation in Europe, but always there was the assumption that Communism was not to be allowed to take over more territory anywhere in the world. There was the fear of China as threatening the independence of her weaker neighbors. It is difficult today for people who did not live through that period to understand why there was so much fear of Communism. There were two things true of Communism at that time that are not true today. The change came between our early involvement in Vietnam as supporters of the French and the beginnings of our direct military intervention. The first was the presence of Stalinism in the Soviet Union. Our leaders may have exaggerated the threat of Stalinism to nations outside the Soviet sphere of influence, but American critics did not exaggerate the horror of Stalin's tyranny in the Soviet Union. In most American minds Communism came to mean Stalinism, and for this reason opposition to Communism had real moral justification. It was not merely a self-serving defense of capitalism; it was also a defense of human rights against an extraordinary combination of technologically structured oppression and sadistic terror.[9] All aspects of Stalinism have not disappeared in the Soviet Union, but a great change did come under Khrushchev and, while his successors are less liberal about intellectual dissent than he was, there is nothing like the systematic terror that prevailed under Stalin.

The other element in the situation in the early 1950's which is not present now was the fact that people in what was called the "free world" felt threatened from both east and west at the same time—by international Communism and especially by the close cooperation of the Soviet Union and China. As I recall that situation, I am not surprised at the extent to which fear of any extension of Communism and further erosion of the "free world" dominated the American policy for two decades. The great misfortune was that neither the passing of Stalinism nor the dissolution of international Communism influenced American policy soon enough to enable our Government to see the folly of intervention in Indochina in order to contain Communism. By the early 1960's it became clear that Communism as an international movement had ceased to be the threat it had once been. There were many national communisms, and it was wholly wrong to equate Communism with Stalinism. If we were eager to limit the power of China, it was ironic that our very policy in Indochina had the effect of weakening an independent Communist nation, North Vietnam, which was determined to resist Chinese domination.

In addition to the American fear of a united international Communism there was an American axiom that Communism was the worst fate that could come to any country, worse than any alternative, though there was seldom any careful examination of alternatives. It was believed to be worse than any corrupt rightist regime, worse than generations of stagnation in poverty, worse than decades of civil war. People in the United States had a right to believe this but they had no right to impose this belief on other countries by fire and sword. Fortunately this belief is losing strength and perhaps the most important experience that has undermined it is the recent American discovery of Communist China. Ten years ago Americans would have been glad to see the destruction of Communism in China even if that would have meant decades of anarchy or a return to the corruption and poverty of the China of the 1940's. Now there is a willingness to admit that China is the only nation that has overcome massive poverty. Also the Chinese people have come to have a social motivation and a concern for the community that is rare in the world, and they have also gained a great deal in morale and in the restoration of their sense of national dignity. If the United States had had its way and had been able to undermine this development in China in the 1950's, this would have been an evil beyond all calculation. Fortunately this did not happen, but the possibility reveals on what morally thin ice our anti-Communism had led us to tread.

This assumption about the evil nature of every form of Communism gave our Government a moral excuse to support a great number of shabby tyrannies around the world, making nonsense of its pretensions to be the defender of anything that could be called the "free world." The phrase came to mean only freedom from Communism. The government in Saigon was and is one of these shabby tyrannies, and its treatment of political prisoners makes it an especially cruel one.

The moral case for containing Communism that at one time had real substance fitted perfectly the desire of the American Government to keep as much of the world as possible open to American economic enterprise. Since ours was the dominant nation after the Second World War, it was a time to use political power to gain markets for American goods and to ensure access to needed raw materials for the American economic system. Pressures within our country for these ends have been immense and they have had the Government on their side. A new generation of revisionist historians interprets American foreign policy since 1945 entirely in terms of American economic imperialism. One of the most authoritative books representing this approach is *The Limits of Power,* by Joyce and Gabriel Kolko (Harper & Row, 1972). I do not doubt that the economic factor was of great importance. However, I think that it was combined with a genuine moral concern about the threat of Stalinism and with a concern for American security against the power of the united Communist nations. These concerns coincided completely with the concerns of those who saw in the extension of Communist power in Europe, Asia, and Latin America a threat to the profits of American corporations abroad and to the American free enterprise system itself.

There may be questions as to who was deceiving whom, but I doubt whether even our leaders would have paid such a price to reach their goals in Indochina if they had been concerned only about American economic interests. Misguided or not, many of them were, I believe, convinced that there was a moral obligation to resist the extension of Communism for the sake of world order as they understood it and for the sake of American security. The idea died hard that if Communism was not stopped in Indochina, it would have to be stopped at some point nearer our shores. Weighing these various factors as they have influenced American policy will be a matter of debate among historians for a long time to come. I have given my impressions based upon my own memory of these events and my participation in them.

ONE MAJOR LESSON

Out of this complex experience in which such tragic mistakes were made and such evil deeds performed in the name of all Americans, I try to emphasize one major lesson. The United States should not use its power to keep other nations from having their own revolutions. The American lid that has been kept on so many situations is generally on the side of rightist tyrannies. Our country began in revolution under almost uniquely favorable conditions and once seemed to be the champion of oppressed people. But its anti-Communism, combined with its tendency toward economic imperialism, has transformed its character and its influence. It is now the great *status quo* power. In the chapter on theologies of liberation I emphasized our role as the opponent of revolutionary change in this hemisphere. That we must abandon this role and free other people to find new ways in their hope for greater justice is one of the chief lessons that should come out of our experience in Indochina.

I am not calling for isolationism. Far from it. Indeed, one of the worst forms of isolationism is to use our power unilaterally as was done in Indochina. Our policy there did not show "a decent respect for the opinions of mankind." I believe that most of those who share the general outlook of this chapter are deeply concerned to strengthen multilateral institutions that have as their center the United Nations. One of the mistakes was to do so little to find ways in which the United Nations might have helped us to end our part in the war in Indochina, perhaps through some new kind of initiative of the General Assembly when the Security Council refused to act.

Also it is the opposite of isolationism to take initiative as a nation to find new ways to overcome world poverty and world hunger. What is needed is a combination of will, inventiveness, and much fresh thinking about reducing the proportion of the world's resources that are consumed by the rich northern nations.

In my early chapters I emphasized the importance of the participation of American churches in the worldwide Christian community as a source of new thoughts and new attitudes in American congregations. This participation is occurring now. I have also emphasized that Christian communities in other parts of the world do not exclusively represent groups of Christians; they also represent their neighbors who are non-Christians, and the needs and destinies of their nations. One wise observer of the younger generation in this country, President Kingman Brewster, Jr., of Yale University, in arguing that our country was not becoming isolationist, had this to say about the students whom he knows so well:

> The current generation does have misgivings about the universal wisdom and virtue of the American experiment and this clashes with the self-righteous scorn for the vicissitudes of the foreigner which has always been such a large part of the isolationist tradition. They are more genuinely imbued with interest in and enthusiasm about peoples, nations, cultures other than their own than any preceding generation of Americans ever has been.[10]

This suggests that there may be unusual resources among our own people that are favorable to the transformation of the American role in the world.

I have already emphasized my belief that our experience of the Indochina war may well be a landmark in the development of the attitude of churches toward war. I shall now give more content to that statement.

Dissent against the Government's policy was probably strongest in women's groups, academic communities, and churches. The established peace organizations were important catalysts. The growth of this dissent in the churches did not differ markedly from its growth in the population as a whole, but I think that we can say that quite early within the churches centers of intense dissent came to exist. As early as 1965 statements by large groups of church leaders began to appear in the press expressing this general position. In 1965 the General Board of the National Council of Churches had begun to question the Government's policy and warned especially that the war would be regarded by the world as a racial war "because we are seen as a predominately white nation using our overwhelming military strength to kill more and more Asians." Clergy and Laity Concerned About Vietnam was founded in 1966 and for a number of years was one of the chief unofficial organizers of religious dissent. Denominations were deeply divided on the subject and there was a tendency in local churches to reflect the views of the surrounding community. After 1967 the dissent grew rapidly partly because of moral revulsion against the destructiveness of American bombing and partly because it was felt that we were failing to achieve our objectives. National spokesmen of many denominations spoke out strongly as individuals and often took part in demonstrations. Radical opposition to the war among Roman Catholics, especially among priests and nuns, was much in the news. The national judicatories of denominations began to speak out after 1970. Among the strongest antiwar statements were those of the General Synod of the United Church of Christ in 1971, of the General Assembly of the United Presbyterian Church in 1970 and 1971, and of the General Conference of The United Methodist Church in 1971. The Roman Catholic bishops as a group in November 1971 declared that the war was unjust because of its disproportionate use of force and also came out for selective conscientious objection and conditional amnesty for draft resisters. This was a climactic event that gave enormous support to dissent. The Jewish community was divided and there was a strong tendency within it to avoid opposing intervention in Indochina because of the possible implications it might have for the defense of Israel. Yet as early as 1967 the Union of American Hebrew Congregations (Reform) took an antiwar stand and this was repeated several times. The American Jewish Congress made a decisive statement in 1972.

As one looks back over this history one sees a pattern. An ecumenical body, the National Council of Churches, was the first of the official bodies to move in this direction. There was a remarkable growth of unofficial opposition to the war which often included the national leaders of denominations from 1965 to the end of major American involvement. The national judicatories of denominations began to move much later, and this was quite natural because of the deep division of opinion in the denominations. Local churches had the greatest difficulty in dealing with the issue, and this again is not strange because of the divisions within them. So many evaded the issue during the Indochina war that there should be fresh thinking now about ways of handling controversial questions that have great moral meaning in local churches. It throws light on this whole development to note that opinion in the country moved in much the same way. The Harris Poll showed in October 1971 that 65 percent of the people at large believed that the war was morally wrong. The difficulty with such a poll is that it does not measure the intensity of convictions and probably most of those who answered in that way were in that year reasonably confident that the President was getting the country out of the war.[11]

From my experience and observation of the broad religious dissent against the war I carry away the impression that there has not been as great an increase of the number of absolute pacifists as one might have expected. I have no statistics to prove this, but my judgment is based in part on the great emphasis on selective conscientious objection that developed during the war. If I am correct there are two

factors that provide some explanation of this situation. One
is that a large number of those who were most opposed to the
war in Indochina are at least open to the possibility that the
use of revolutionary violence in some situations may be justified. Here I am stressing openness rather than outright
advocacy, but that is sufficient to make it difficult to embrace
absolute pacifism. The other factor is that a great many people who remember the Second World War would still have
difficulty in saying that the use of military force against the
power of Hitler was not justified. Similarly there are those
who shared in the dissent against the Indochina war, but who
cannot reject the moral right of Israel to defend her existence however they may criticize elements of intransigence
in the policy of her government. There is a background condition that should be mentioned: the strong tendency to go
some distance with "situationism" in ethics, to recognize the
uniqueness and also the unpredictability of situations even
when there would be considerable criticism of Joseph Fletcher's "situation ethics" as a total position.

The effect of our experience of the Indochina war combined with the realization of what a nuclear war would be,
even if it does not cause people to become absolute pacifists,
will set narrower limits than ever before to the wars that can
be justified. Nuclear war or war that is likely to escalate into
nuclear war would be outside those limits. The same would
be true of an ideological war of intervention by a great power
to impose its will on weaker nations—such as the Indochina
war. I have already referred to the statement of the Second
Vatican Council about wars against populations and to the
statement of the Uppsala Assembly of the World Council of
Churches about nuclear war. These statements and the very
widespread opinion that supports them do not solve the
problem created by the fact that nuclear armaments exist
and threaten the human race. They do not imply that a
monopoly of nuclear power should be allowed to exist in any
nation or group of nations. They do imply that adventurous

initiatives to reduce armaments even unilaterally are essential. The fact that reliance on nuclear deterrence coincided with the absolute enmity of the cold war should spur governments, beginning with our own, to take advantage of the dissolution of absolute enmity to seek alternatives to deterrence based upon the absolute weapon. There is too much complacency in the face of the dreadful fact that our Government's missiles and those of the Soviet Union are aimed at populations. To use them to destroy populations would be, as Vatican II said, "a crime against God and man himself." The ethics of nuclear armaments as well as of nuclear war needs to come back into the center of attention.

If my argument so far is along right lines, I believe that we are now in a situation in which the relation between churches and governments must be reversed. On matters of war and peace churches have given the benefit of the doubt to governments since they were supposed to be in the know and they had responsibility to act quickly to defend a nation's security. Today, must we not say that the burden of proof is on governments, because even those who are not pacifists are driven to the conclusion that any war is likely to be unjustified? This is a position on which Protestants and Catholics can unite. It is supported by one of the bitterest experiences of recent years, the discovery that the American Government has consistently deceived the American people about the realities of the war in Indochina, about the military operations in Laos, about the bombing of Cambodia prior to the announced invasion of that country by "our side," and, most fateful of all, about the attacks by the South Vietnamese under our auspices on the North Vietnamese coast near the Gulf of Tonkin before the alleged attacks by the North Vietnamese on our ships that were the occasion of the Tonkin Gulf resolution that was used by the president to justify American belligerency.[12]

In many other countries today the conflicts between church and state are generally over basic human rights. The emergence of the church as the most articulate champion of

those rights in many nations is one of the most significant
facts about the church in our time. In the United States the
Bill of Rights in the federal constitution is a great resource
and, while there will be conflicts over these rights as there
were in the days of Joseph McCarthy, it is not in this context
that the chief tension between church and state is experienced here. Alan Paton, writing in the South African
situation, in which elements in the church are today in a
profound conflict with the state (and also, unfortunately, with
other elements in the church), says that the South African
problem is the worse "because we have no constitution (to
speak of) and no bill of rights."[13] In this country the major
tension between church and state is likely to be over the
war-making power of the state. Indeed, conflicts over human
rights are likely once again to arise—conflicts over the rights
of those who object to military service on conscientious
grounds, including selective conscientious objectors. The
churches in this country as units of a universal Christian
community have a different perspective from that of the
state, and this should come to modify more than it has ever
done the attitudes of Christian citizens. Often the conflict
may be not with the state as such but with the administration
in power, as the latter takes initiative for foreign and military
policy, sometimes being checked by Congress. Also I should
explain that when I speak of tension or conflict between
church and state I do not envisage a consensus within the
whole church as an ecclesiastical community; rather, I see
the church as a sounding board for many forms of witness by
Christian groups and individuals and often this witness, as in
the case of the dissent on Vietnam, would have strong support from national spokesmen and agencies of the church.

A Second Look at Civil Religion

Much has been said recently about the American "civil
religion." Robert Bellah's influential article[14] on that subject
gave a considerable impetus to this interest. I had been in-

clined to dismiss civil religion as a form of idolatry or at least of that less explicit idolatry which assumes that God—even the God worshiped in churches and synagogues—is on the side of this nation. I think that this form of idolatry is always in the line of least resistance because of the power of nationalism over the consciences of citizens.

Senator Mark Hatfield, in a speech that became quite famous at a prayer breakfast in Washington attended by Richard Nixon and Billy Graham and 3,000 others on January 31, 1973, warned against "the god of civil religion." He said:

> If we leaders appeal to the god of civil religion, our faith is in a small and exclusive deity, a loyal spiritual adviser to power and prestige, a defender only of the American nation, the object of a national folk religion devoid of moral content. But if we pray to the Biblical God of justice and righteousness, we fall under God's judgment for calling upon his name but failing to obey his commands.

Since the senator was known to be one of the chief opponents of the American war policy it was an unusual event when he implied so clearly in the presence of the governmental elite that this was an aspect of "the sin that has scarred our national soul." The occasion was an example of the kind of ritual that usually celebrates the national god.

Yet, as Bellah has emphasized, at its best the American civil religion does point to the transcendent, even to divine judgment upon the nation as this was expressed by Abraham Lincoln. Bellah sees great significance in the words of John F. Kennedy when in his inaugural address he three times mentioned the name of God. His oath of office was sworn before God as well as before the people. He said: "The rights of man come not from the generosity of the state but from the hand of God." Kennedy concluded with the words: "Here on earth God's work must truly be our own." This could all be dismissed as pious rhetoric that has behind it political expediency. But, it need not be dismissed in that way. That it seemed fitting for a president—and one of our more sophisticated presidents—to speak to the people about God as transcending the national will even so vaguely does suggest that there are symbolic pointers to God's judgment and providence in the civil religion to which churches and synagogues can give far more meaning than civil religion as such encompasses. This meaning would not be imposed in any way upon those who have neither Christian nor Jewish commitments, but it could be for them a carrier of ethical insight that their consciences would accept. The most important element in this meaning that has Biblical sources for our purpose here is that God is the God of all nations and has no favorites among them. "Did I not bring up Israel from the land of Egypt, and the Philistines from Caphtor and the Syrians from Kir?" (Amos 9:7.)

More important than even the best words of presidents is the fact that our nation recognizes the authority of a Constitution by which those who have most power in government are judged and that has within it pointers to moral standards that partake of the transcendent. When courts appeal to the "equal protection" clause they point to a moral absolute, even though there will always be a great deal of relativistic balancing in the ways it is applied. Equality is an ideal that is never satisfied. There are always neglected groups of people who have not yet had the benefits of equal justice, and there are always forms of disadvantage of which existing laws do not fully take account. Another pointer to a transcendent judgment that has special significance today is the prohibition of "cruel and unusual punishments." One of the worst sins of governments is their propensity to inflict cruel punishments, and this is especially true today in the case of political dissenters in many countries. American courts are now struggling with the question as to whether or not capital punishment is a violation of this clause. Whatever may be decided in the near future, it is of great importance that decisions on this issue are made under the judgment of this high standard.

The same can be said of other First Amendment rights. Judges differ, and will continue to differ, as they balance these rights with other claims upon them, but they can never escape the moral pressure that is present in the First Amendment. The story of the United States Supreme Court's struggle with the claims of Jehovah's Witnesses that their children had the right to abstain from saluting the flag is a fascinating illustration of this balancing, and also in the end of the power of the constitutional guarantee of the right to religious liberty. In an opinion written by Justice Felix Frankfurter in 1940, the court denied this claim in the interest of national unity, but Justice Harlan Stone in a stirring minority opinion wrote: "I am not prepared to say that the right of this small and helpless minority, including children having a strong religious conviction, whether they understand its nature or not, to refrain from an expression obnoxious to their religion, is to be overborne by the interest of the state in maintaining discipline in the schools." In 1943 the court reversed itself and the minority opinion of (then) Chief Justice Stone became the substance of the majority opinion. Between 1940 and 1943 there was an intense national argument among legal authorities in which other courts were involved. One sees in this the power of the First Amendment as applied to the rights of a tiny, helpless minority to win its way with the legal establishment even in time of war. There could be no better demonstration of the reality of the process built into the American constitutional system by which existing governmental powers are under a judgment that may well transcend their own conscious moral commitments. This reality gives much substance to civil religion and often preserves it from becoming national idolatry. Chief Justice Charles Evans Hughes, in his famous dissent in the Macintosh case in 1931, said: "One cannot speak of religious liberty, with proper appreciation of its essential and historic significance, without assuming the existence of a belief in supreme allegiance to the will of God."

There will be conflicts between church and state, but to some degree the church can appeal to the state's own traditions and to its own supreme law. That this is the case is a great moral resource and for me it is a ground for affirming American patriotism. The purging of the national religiosity from national idolatry will be a continual struggle but not a hopeless one. When there is conflict between church and state over the use of military power or of covert operations on other continents to maintain, in the American interest, a shockingly unjust *status quo,* or when there is a conflict over the military readiness to destroy populations, the most important word of witness will be this: The victims of injustice and the targeted populations are people loved of God, people to whom all Americans are tied with bonds of human solidarity. God's judgment and mercy are for all peoples together.

VIII
Facing the Global Threats
to Humanity

In this concluding chapter I shall suggest a framework from which we may face the many new interlocking threats to humanity. Several times in this book I have mentioned that I have lived through three different periods. The first was one of uncritical optimism, of the assumption that though progress was not necessarily inevitable, one could have confidence in the future through the extension of Western civilization, the improvement of education, and the growth of democracy. The second period began after the First World War. It included facing such monstrous evils as Hitlerism and Stalinism, and the coming of the Second World War. It included the first use of nuclear bombs, and the recognition of the possibility of general nuclear annihilation. In a few years many of us moved from simple hopes to fears even for humanity's survival. At least in the United States and also in the Third World there was to some extent a revival of the earlier hopes toward the end of the 1950's. Then the civil rights movement in its early days seemed to suggest a new dawn; people in the Third World rebelled against the tired Western "realism" that seemed to deny them a good future. Today, in a fourth period, a new pattern of fear has emerged. New threats to humanity that did not enter into consciousness during the second period, the period of theological realism, are now very much in our minds.

It is the interlocking aspect of these new threats which is most disturbing. Robert Heilbroner, in a most provocative article on "The Human Prospect,"[1] has helped to crystallize the ideas about this pattern of threats. I shall summarize in my own way some of the elements in this pattern.

There is the prospect of an increase in population that will outstrip the food supply and other resources and in some countries will leave too little space per person and make most problems less manageable politically, socially, and economically. There is a growing awareness of the finiteness of resources, including food and energy. Indeed in regard to both there is already an emergency. I have emphasized the present reality of hunger and famine in several parts of the world. There is also the vulnerability of the environment— the air, the water, and the earth itself, even the oceans—to many kinds of pollution. This vulnerability also sets limits to the *use* of resources. It sets limits to the disposal of waste and, according to some speculations, to the amount of energy-produced heat that can be absorbed. It follows logically that scarcity will aggravate many kinds of conflicts between nations and peoples. There is still the threat of nuclear annihilation, which will increase with the spread of nuclear weapons. There is the danger that wars may start through the use of military force to gain control of scarce resources. We are told that such a use of force is not now planned in the case of oil, but the prospect is denied in ways that suggest it as a possibility. There is the difficulty of establishing governments that are strong enough to govern effectively and yet are able to leave room for personal freedom, for the human rights of the Bill of Rights. This is an ancient problem, but it is immensely aggravated by the need to establish new political systems under conditions of great stress. Abraham Lincoln stated the perennial problem when he said: "Must a government, of necessity, be too strong for the liberties of its own people, or too weak to maintain its existence?" Much more than the existence of a government is at stake. A government must be able to solve problems that boggle the mind.

Hunger, war, and tyranny may be the human prospect if all these tendencies continue without check, without countervailing tendencies not yet in sight. There is even the possibility that the earth itself may become unfit for human habitation.

I am sure there could be many arguments about each of these statements. Today the limits-of-growth proposal has stimulated a great debate, especially among people in the poorer countries that obviously need growth. This very idea is sometimes regarded as a kind of plot of the rich to keep the poor from rising. It may be better to speak of the limits of resources because it so obviously applies to the rich countries and to their need to cut back on their use of them. Many countries must continue to have economic growth. Whatever the arguments, there is enough in what I have projected to call for our hardest thinking.

I shall outline four elements in the frame of faith from which I believe that we today should face this troubled future. I shall have occasion from time to time to refer to ideas already stated in earlier chapters to relate them to this frame. The relationship of these four elements to each other is of special importance.

1. First, when we attempt as Christians to get our bearings, we should begin with the confession of faith that the world and all its people, including ourselves and the whole human prospect, are under God as revealed to us in Christ. God is no vague Supreme Being or Almighty but central aspects of his nature and purpose are revealed. In ways that are mysterious he combines both power and love.

We must not use this confession as a pious shortcut to a cheap hope or to the end of thought. Yet, if humanity is not alone, this makes all the difference as we face an uncertain future. One of the verses that helps me most as we face our personal destinies is Paul's great sentence: "If we live, we live to the Lord, and if we die, we die to the Lord; so then,

whether we live or whether we die, we are the Lord's" (Rom.
14:8). What those words may mean for the whole human race
may not be clear, but they are a way of saying that humanity
is not alone in an alien environment, and in the end that may
be the most meaningful expression of faith.

In practical terms this confession means at least the following: *(a)* that we avoid panic and an ultimate fear; and *(b)* that
we see the future as partly open.

The future is not fully open. We cannot regard it as though
nuclear weapons had never been made. It cannot be as
though increase of population had not already gathered dangerous momentum. Judging from past experience we may be
sure of one thing: predictions of the long-term future are
most precarious and must not be allowed to limit our vision.
Self-fulfilling prophecies should be avoided.

We do not hold up the world like Atlas, but we do have
very important responsibilities. Because of our role in our
time and place, if some things are not done by us they will
not be done at all. But what we do should be accompanied
by humility. How responsibility can go with humility without
being undercut by it may be another mystery, but we need
not give up on it. There is no excuse to escape doing what we
can do. We cannot deny that American citizens have a degree of freedom to act in ways that can influence national
decisions; nor can we deny that our nation is entrusted with
enormous wealth and power, the use of which will be most
fateful for humanity's future.

2. My second suggestion is that the very sources of our most
harassing problems contain signs of both divine judgment
and divine providence. These do not work out neatly. They
never do. Even the most obvious examples of divine judgment are confused by the suffering of the innocent, often
their massive suffering. And even the most promising providential new beginnings are easily marred by pride and often
by an irrational fanaticism that perpetuates cruel conflict.

To get a fresh view of this dimension of our history, I have tried to put myself in the place of the people who had most power in the world in an earlier period: from about 1900 to 1914. I have been helped in this by Barbara Tuchman's remarkable book, *The Proud Tower*,[2] which is a vivid description of the people in Western Europe and in North America who at that time believed that they had the world and its future in their control, living as they did in their proud tower. They did not control themselves very well, as their follies got them into the First World War. Looking out from their proud tower they saw that most of Asia and Africa was under their domination. The world appeared to them to be relatively stable. Those among them who were idealists believed that Western civilization was the greatest secular good and that eventually other parts of the world would greatly benefit from its extension. Churches were confident that the evangelization of "lesser breeds without the Law" would make them more like Western Christians.

Yet most of humanity in those days was in a condition of subjection. Injustice was everywhere and its victims were hardly able to protest effectively. Their voices had not yet begun to be heard. Even the most powerful people in the proud tower had just begun to pay attention to the victims of injustice in their own countries. How could they be expected even to see the victims on other continents—for these belonged to strange races and to strange cultures? There was an Anglo-Saxon, northern European racism that was blinding. The United States was just beginning to get into the imperialistic act affecting distant peoples. One president took the Philippines, as he said, for their good. Another president used his "big stick" to take Panama, doubtless for the sake of our national security.

Why do I go into all of this? To make one point. I think that it is better to live in the world as it is with all of its problems than it would be to live in that proud tower where people had so many illusions about themselves and about most of humanity. Their world was so full of helpless, inarticulate people who were victims of injustice and were hardly seen.

The stability that comforted them was a fraud. I referred to signs of divine judgment and divine providence. These can be seen in the liquidation of the great empires and in the rising of neglected and oppressed people to claim independence and to put us on the moral defensive—perhaps in spite of ourselves. In our country there was the rising of industrial workers, of blacks, of farm workers, and now of women.

Now, a question: Is it not likely that, while we do not have all the illusions that people in the proud tower had in 1900, there is a similar false relationship between the people in the affluent northern nations, including our own, and the people in countries that are impoverished, in which there are a billion or more hungry or malnourished people who even now are visited by or threatened by famine? Is it not likely that those in future generations who look back upon us in our tower of affluence, which is not without its pride, will make judgments about our wealth and economic imperialism that will be similar to those that we make today about the political domination of northern white people in 1900?

In an earlier chapter I quoted the passionate statement of Archbishop Helder Câmara, addressed to us who live in the northern hemisphere, in which he referred to the need for overcoming the egoism of the northern hemisphere. Part of the experience of being members of the worldwide Christian community is that today we are often addressed in this way with utmost frankness by our fellow Christians in other situations who speak to us not only for themselves but also for their nations and peoples.

I have referred to our more indirect economic imperialism, but we have also directly used military power in a brutal way in Indochina. We also have a habit of using the C.I.A. directly to impose our Government's political will on other countries, as was done in Chile. I do not know how it may come, but in the next period there should be a vast upheaval comparable to the end of the political forms of imperial domination.

There is a question as to how radical change can occur

without so undermining the economies in the northern countries that there will be general stagnation and more poverty and hunger for the people who most need change. Within our own country it is difficult to focus on the problems of global injustice because people feel threatened by inflation or unemployment. Americans may be in some kind of tower, but from within it seems to be a leaning tower.

These difficulties are real enough, but within the Christian community—and I am not claiming that the Christian community has any monopoly on moral sensitivity in these matters—there needs to be the beginning of a reversal of the generally accepted attitudes and axioms. A self-examination and a self-discipline that will prepare a great many Americans to move toward ways of life that do not depend on consuming 40 percent of the world's resources must begin. There needs to be recognition now of the religious hypocrisy, of the moral scandal, and of the sheer irrationality of the present ordering of the world for our economic advantage. This should become a part of our everyday consciousness.

3. My third suggestion is that we take seriously some elements in Christian teaching about humanity. It makes a great difference if we see the world from the standpoint of faith—an understanding that greatly emphasizes the full humanity of all persons as made by God in his own image and as revealed in their dignity by Christ. This is no platitude. It means that there are no "gooks"; that there are no "lesser breeds without the Law"; that the billion or more people who are most threatened in our world are one with ourselves and we with them. This has not usually been clearly seen even in the churches. I have referred to the Anglo-Saxon, northern European racism that has really controlled attitudes; this has lost its respectability, and none of us will admit that we are influenced by it. Our faith does not in a simple way exalt humanity as virtuous, for we also learn from it about the depth and stubbornness of sin, of pride and egoism and sloth. Yet there is one very important aspect of Christian

teaching about this less hopeful side of humanity. It should never be a reason for running down another people, because when we talk about sin we should begin with our own sin in confession and not with that of another segment of humanity.

I have quoted Henry Ward Beecher's statement that "no man in this land suffers from poverty unless it be more than his fault—unless it be his sin." What a way of using Christian teaching about sin to put others in their "place," and how comforting for the comfortable! People cannot say such things today without making themselves ridiculous. If we could in principle despair of most people, especially of those most unlike ourselves, the world would indeed be a hopeless place. Think how a few years ago we despaired of the whole Chinese nation, and they probably despaired of us. I do not claim that we can deduce solutions from this teaching, but it is the right angle from which we should look for solutions.

4. My fourth emphasis has endless ramifications and I can only point to it by means of a few random illustrations. I have in mind the unpredictable breakthroughs of movements of the Spirit, sometimes in religious and sometimes in secular guise. These breakthroughs, first seen in what we may call sacred history, have extraordinary effects in secular history. If the story of humanity were told leaving out the influence of the prophets of Israel and of the first-century events in Palestine associated with Jesus Christ, it would be a great distortion. Even Bertrand Russell, who had so little use for traditional religions, in his fine book *Power,* said: "If I were to select four men who have had more power than any others, I should mention Buddha, Christ, Pythagoras, Galileo."[3] Paul, who was close to those events in time, could not have imagined the ways in which his words were to come true: "God chose what is low and despised in the world, even things that are not, to bring to nothing things that are" (I Cor. 1:28).

Consider the following passage, which comes from no

Christian apologist, but from the French philosopher Henri Bergson. He has been speaking about the fact that Stoic philosophers taught that all men are brothers. Then he says:

> Humanity had to wait till Christianity for the idea of universal brotherhood, with its implication of equality of rights and the sanctity of the person, to become operative. Some may say that it has been rather a slow process; indeed centuries elapsed before the rights of man were proclaimed by the Puritans of America, soon followed by the men of the French Revolution. It began, nevertheless, with the teachings of the Gospels, and was destined to go on indefinitely; it is one thing for an idea to be merely propounded by sages worthy of admiration, it is very different when the idea is broadcast to the ends of the earth in a message overflowing with love, invoking love in return.[4]

Let the reader discount that statement as he may choose. It comes from an evolutionary cast of mind that was more hopeful than ours today. It is too Western in its orientation. It reminds us of a Christian triumphalism that is now widely rejected, though the author was not a Christian when he wrote those words.[5] Yet there is an important core of truth in them. The influence of the gospel has broken through many walls of partition; it has created new realities not only in the church but also in the world, and it has created new possibilities that remain ahead of us. Those words, "when the idea is broadcast to the ends of the earth in a message overflowing with love, invoking love in return," tell us about something of great moment that has happened in human history. The gospel has indeed had global echoes. Today this may not be taken very seriously; perhaps we may come to give weight to it again if we allow ourselves to imagine what the world would be like if it had never happened.

Consider some examples of recent movements of the Spirit that have had influence on secular history. There was the influence of Pope John (who was expected to do no more than conduct a holding operation) on his church and beyond, even to some extent on the cold war as a spiritual conflict. After him the "holy war" against Communism had little support, and without this development there could be little hope for peace or even for human survival. The remarkable transformations in the church in Latin America are a miracle of the Spirit. Who would have guessed only a short time ago that in country after country today the church would be the greatest defender of human rights, not only of the rights of the church or of Christians but also the rights of all humanity. I have emphasized this in an earlier chapter. It seems that churches under pressure still surprise because of their strength and their capacity to rise to the occasion. In this country little is expected of the church, but it would be well to look abroad and see what the church can be.

There was more power in the early days of the civil rights movement—as it was represented by Martin Luther King, Jr. —to put white people all over the nation on the moral defensive than is now recognized, because of continuing frustrations. I hate to think what the situation would be like now if there had not been a considerable change both in the consciences of white people and in the self-confidence and courage of black people as a result of that movement of the Spirit.

In the 1960's there was a movement of the Spirit among a great many young people that took the form of a rejection of many aspects of the materialism of our culture and also a rejection of racism. This movement also did much to form the deeper level of dissent against the war in Indochina. It was a complete rejection of national chauvinism, and it involved a remarkable openness to people of other nations and cultures. I doubt if it has been followed by a return to uncritical materialism, to racism, or to chauvinism today. There were consciously Christian elements in this movement of the Spirit, there were other religious elements, and there was much in it that had no direct religious source. But this does not matter. What does matter is that persons with this new outlook will have considerable influence in the future on the public policies of our nation. This will be important both for reconciliation between nations that are armed against each other and whose governments are still partly controlled by the spirit of the cold war. It will also be important when there are new patterns forced upon the nation, so that it may consume less of the world's resources.

I conclude by emphasizing the importance of holding together these four elements in the frame of faith and thought from which we should view the future. If we had only the fourth element, the movements of the Spirit that are recognizable as such, there might be no more to be expected than the existence of small minorities and remnants that would have little chance to influence historical trends. If we had only the second, the signs of judgment and providence that are most visible, we might expect chiefly catastrophes that would leave history strewn with the wreckage of proud towers. It is because we also have the first, faith in God's rule (in spite of appearances), and because we have the third, faith that all human beings have dignity and are capable of receiving directly and indirectly under many names the influences of the Spirit (this also in spite of appearances), that we may live in the world with hope for future embodiments in history of justice and reconciliation.

Notes

Chapter I. SOURCES OF THE RADICAL IMPERATIVE

1. William Temple, *Nature, Man and God* (The Macmillan Company, 1934), p. 478.
2. Karl Barth, *Church Dogmatics* (Edinburgh: T. & T. Clark, 1957), Vol. II, Part I, p. 386.
3. Karl Barth, "The Christian Community and the Civil Community," in *Against the Stream* (London: S.C.M. Press, 1934), p. 36.
4. Dorothee Soelle, *Political Theology,* tr. by John Shelley (Fortress Press, 1974), Ch. 7.
5. Walter Rauschenbusch, *A Theology for the Social Gospel* (The Macmillan Company, 1917), p. 79.
6. *Ibid.,* p. 43.
7. Reinhold Niebuhr, *Beyond Tragedy* (Charles Scribner's Sons, 1937), p. 81.
8. Helder Câmara. From *Cross Currents,* Summer 1970.
9. Walter Rauschenbusch, *Christianity and the Social Crisis* (The Macmillan Company, 1907), p. 46.

Chapter II. BIBLICAL SOURCES OF ETHICAL GUIDANCE

1. Reinhold Niebuhr, *The Nature and Destiny of Man* (Charles Scribner's Sons, 1943), Vol. II, p. 74.
2. Günther Bornkamm, *Jesus of Nazareth,* tr. by Irene and Fraser McLuskey (Harper & Row, Publishers, Inc., 1961).
3. W. D. Davies, *Invitation to the New Testament* (Doubleday & Company, Inc., 1966), p. 135.
4. H. Shelton Smith, *In His Image, But...: Racism in Southern Religion, 1780–1910* (Duke University Press, 1972).
5. John Woolman, *Journal,* Ch. IV.

6. *The National Catholic Reporter,* March 29, 1974.

7. Abraham Heschel, *The Prophets* (The Burning Bush Press, 1962), pp. 271-272.

8. S.G.F. Brandon, *Jesus and the Zealots* (Manchester University Press, 1967).

9. Oscar Cullmann, *Jesus and the Revolutionaries,* tr. by Gareth Putnam (Harper and Row, Publishers, Inc., 1970).

10. Oscar Cullmann, *The State in the New Testament* (Charles Scribner's Sons, 1956).

11. Cullmann, *Jesus and the Revolutionaries,* pp. 27-28.

12. *Ibid.,* p. 14.

13. Rauschenbusch, *A Theology for the Social Gospel,* p. 258.

14. John Howard Yoder's *The Politics of Jesus* (Wm. B. Eerdmans Publishing Company, 1972) is extremely helpful in bringing together those aspects of the life and teachings of Jesus that have political implications for our time. The fact that he is an absolute pacifist of Mennonite convictions gives him a sharp eye for support for pacifism in the Gospels. I have problems in deducing even a pacifist political strategy from the teachings of Jesus, but I know full well that they put a heavy burden of proof on anyone who feels justified in using violence against any other person. It is not strange that many Christians make no sense of the claim that there are situations in which the use of violence can be justified. Yoder's book has on its jacket: "Love your enemies, do good to those who hate you; bless those who curse you and pray for those who maltreat you." To me those words are of deeper significance and more universally applicable than words about nonviolence, and it should be a test of the faithfulness of the Christian and of the church as to whether or not they remain at all times the overruling guidance.

15. Joseph Fletcher, *Situation Ethics* (The Westminster Press, 1966), p. 25.

16. *Ibid.,* p. 98.

Chapter III. FORMS OF CORPORATE ETHICAL GUIDANCE

1. Karl Barth made use of this criterion within a passage in which there was a clear reference to the government of Hitler. He wrote as follows: "It could well be that we could obey specific rulers only by being disobedient to God and by being thus disobedient to the political order ordained by God as well. It could well be that we had to do with a Government of liars, murderers and incendiaries, with a Government which wished to usurp the place of God, to fetter the conscience, to suppress the church and become itself the

Church of Antichrist." He is here describing Hitler's government as he was known to feel about it, and I have always considered the reference to incendiaries to be a reference to the Reichstag fire. Barth links this event very closely to the example of John Knox and the Scottish Confession of 1560. See his *The Knowledge of God and the Service of God* (Gifford Lectures), tr. by J.L.M. Haire and Ian Henderson (Charles Scribner's Sons, 1939).

2. Dorothee Soelle, *Political Theology*, p. 37.

3. *The Lambeth Conferences—1867-1948.* Section on the Lambeth Conference of 1948, Report on the Church and the Modern World, Part 2, p. 21.

4. Reinhold Niebuhr, *Pious and Secular America* (Charles Scribner's Sons, 1958), p. 108.

5. Charles Y. Glock and Rodney Stark, *Christian Beliefs and Anti-Semitism* (Harper and Row, Publishers, Inc., Harper Torchbooks, 1966); Rodney Stark *et al.*, *Wayward Shepherds: Prejudice and the Protestant Clergy* (Harper and Row, Publishers, Inc., 1971).

6. Reported to the men of the Bryn Mawr Presbyterian Church, Bryn Mawr, Pennsylvania, by Robert H. Hilpert, May 7, 1967.

7. Paul Ramsey, *Who Speaks for the Church? A Critique of the 1966 Geneva Conference on Church and Society* (Abingdon Press, 1967).

8. *Ibid.*, p. 67.

9. *Ibid.*, p. 82.

10. *The Ecumenical Review*, Oct. 1973.

11. Roger Shinn, "The Impact of Science and Technology on the Theological Understanding of Social Justice," *Anticipation* (published by the World Council of Churches), May 1974.

12. Samuel L. Parmar, in *The Ecumenical Review*, Jan. 1974, p. 44.

13. The report of the World Council of Churches study on "The Future of Man and Society in a World of Science-based Technology" was published in *Anticipation*, Nov. 1974.

Chapter IV. THE CONFLICT IN AMERICAN CHURCHES OVER
SOCIAL ETHICS

1. Reinhard Bendix, *Max Weber—An Intellectual Portrait* (Doubleday & Company, Inc., Anchor Books, 1962), p. 247.

2. *Ibid.*, p. 265.

3. Max Weber, *The Protestant Ethic and the Spirit of Capitalism*, tr. by Talcott Parsons (Charles Scribner's Sons, 1930), p. 175.

4. Sydney E. Ahlstrom, *A Religious History of the American*

People (Yale University Press, 1972), pp. 789–790. Readers will find more evidence of this tendency gathered together in the chapter entitled "The Gospel of Wealth of the Gilded Age" in Ralph Henry Gabriel's *The Course of American Democratic Thought: An Intellectual History Since 1815* (The Ronald Press Company, 1940).

5. Martin E. Marty, *Righteous Empire: The Protestant Experience in America* (The Dial Press, Inc., 1970), pp. 144–145.

6. Reinhold Niebuhr, *Moral Man and Immoral Society* (Charles Scribner's Sons, 1932), p. 91.

7. Jeffrey K. Hadden, *The Gathering Storm in the Churches: A Sociologist's View of the Widening Gap Between Clergy and Laymen* (Doubleday & Company, Inc., 1969).

8. *Ibid.*, p. 141.

9. Rodney Stark *et al.*, *Wayward Shepherds* (Harper & Row, Publishers, Inc., 1971).

10. *Ibid.*, p. 111.

11. Dean M. Kelley, *Why Conservative Churches Are Growing: A Study in Sociology of Religion* (Harper & Row, Publishers, Inc., 1972).

12. See the article by Seymour M. Hersh in *The New York Times*, Sept. 8, 1974, which has been confirmed by subsequent revelations.

13. *The New York Times*, June 6, 1974.

14. Richard Quebedeaux, *The Young Evangelicals: Revolution in Orthodoxy* (Harper & Row, Publishers, Inc., 1974). The significance of the book by Quebedeaux may be seen in the fact that *Christianity Today*, the chief organ of conservative evangelicalism, published a five-page review of it as its leading article on April 26, 1974. The review was written by former editor Carl F. H. Henry, who is one of the chief scholars and elder statesmen of the movement. Henry did not challenge the facts presented about the "young evangelicals," though he disagreed with some of their conclusions. He agrees with some of the protests of this younger group against the social positions of their predecessors. This is indicated not only by some of his comments in the review but also by the fact that he signed the Chicago Declaration of November 1973, from which I have quoted.

15. *Ibid.*, p. 82.

16. Charles Y. Glock *et al.*, *To Comfort and to Challenge: A Dilemma of the Contemporary Church* (University of California Press, 1967).

17. H. Richard Niebuhr, *The Kingdom of God in America* (Willett, Clark & Company, 1937), p. 193.

18. Herbert Butterfield, *Christianity and History* (Charles Scrib-

ner's Sons, 1950), p. 41. This is a favorite theme of Butterfield and it is developed in the context of international relations in his *Christianity, Diplomacy and War* (Abingdon-Cokesbury Press, 1953).

Chapter V. THEOLOGIES OF LIBERATION

1. Rosemary Radford Ruether, *Liberation Theology: Human Hope Confronts Christian History and American Power* (Paulist/Newman Press, 1972), p. 95.

2. Phyllis Trible, who makes this point, has written one of the most authoritative discussions of these issues in her article "Depatriarchalizing in Biblical Interpretation" in *The Journal of the American Academy of Religion* (March 1973).

3. Dietrich Bonhoeffer, *Letter and Papers from Prison,* ed. by Eberhard Bethge, enlarged edition (The Macmillan Company, 1972), pp. 43–44. It is true that in his earlier writings Bonhoeffer does have a strongly authoritarian and patriarchal side to his thought.

4. Krister Stendahl discusses this in a booklet, *The Bible and the Role of Women.* (Fortress Press, 1966). The subtitle is "A Case Study in Hermeneutics." It was originally written during a controversy over the ordination of women in the Church of Sweden. At the time all but one of the New Testament scholars in the Swedish universities opposed the ordination of women as inconsistent with the thought of the New Testament. Stendahl sought to counteract that position and he was finally successful.

5. "Woman in Mediaeval Theology" by Eleanor Commo McLaughlin, in *Religion and Sexism: Images of Woman in the Jewish and Christian Traditions,* ed. by Rosemary Radford Ruether (Simon & Schuster, Inc., 1974), pp. 226–227. This volume is an excellent expression of the ferment on these issues in theological schools. Similar volumes are *Sexist Religion and Women in the Church,* ed. by Alice L. Hageman (Association Press, 1974); and *Women in a Strange Land,* ed. by Clare Fischer, *et al.* (Fortress Press, 1975).

6. A helpful discussion of both Abbott and Rauschenbusch is Dorothy Bass Fraser's article "The Feminine Mystique: 1890–1910" in *The Union Seminary Quarterly Review* (Summer 1972).

7. Cleveland's article is reprinted in *The Woman Movement: Feminism in the U.S. and England,* ed. by William L. O'Neill (Quadrangle Books, Inc., 1971) pp. 158–163.

8. Dorothy L. Sayers, *Are Women Human?* (Wm. B. Eerdmans Publishing Company, 1971), pp. 24–25.

9. James H. Cone, *A Black Theology of Liberation* (J. B. Lippincott Company, 1970), p. 31.

10. There is a very helpful article on "Social Gospel Christianity and Racism" by Glenn R. Bucher in *The Union Seminary Quar'erly Review*, Winter 1973.

11. Rauschenbusch, *A Theology for the Social Gospel* (The Macmillan Company, 1917), p. 79.

12. Benjamin E. Mays, *Born to Rebel: An Autobiography* (Charles Scribner's Sons, 1971), p. 75.

13. *Ibid.*, p. 241.

14. John Mbiti, "An African Views American Black Theology," *Worldview*, August 1974.

15. Cone, *A Black Theology of Liberation*, p. 119.

16. *Ibid.*, p. 19.

17. *Ibid.*, p. 21.

18. James H. Cone, *Black Theology and Black Power* (The Seabury Press, Inc., 1969), p. 1.

19. *Ibid.*, p. 69.

20. Albert B. Cleage, Jr., *The Black Messiah* (Sheed & Ward, Inc., 1969).

21. Cone, *A Black Theology of Liberation*, pp. 28 and 32.

22. *Ibid.*, p. 25.

23. *Ibid.*, p. 26.

24. *Ibid.*, p. 174.

25. *Ibid.*, p. 190.

26. *Ibid.*, p. 100.

27. *Ibid.*, p. 193.

28. Gustavo Gutiérrez, *A Theology of Liberation: History, Politics and Salvation*, tr. and ed. by Sr. Caridad Inda and John Eagleson (Orbis Books, 1973).

29. *Ibid.*, p. 88.

30. *Ibid.*, pp. 64–65.

31. See *ibid.*, pp. 36–37.

32. *Ibid.*, p. 273.

33. *Ibid.*

34. *Ibid.*, p. 89.

35. *When All Else Fails: Christian Arguments on Violent Revolution*, ed. by IDO-C (The Pilgrim Press, 1970), p. 174.

36. Gutiérrez, *A Theology of Liberation*, p. 276.

37. Paulo Freire, *Pedagogy of the Oppressed*, tr. by Myra Bergman Ramos (Herder & Herder, Inc., 1970), p. 28.

38. Gutiérrez, *A Theology of Liberation*, p. 233.

39. *Ibid.*, p. 238.

40. *Ibid.*

Chapter VI. A RETURN TO ECONOMIC ETHICS

1. Emil Brunner, *The Divine Imperative*, tr. by Olive Wyon (The Westminster Press, 1947), p. 423. This book was first published in German in 1932.

2. These references to the Oxford Conference can be found in *The Oxford Conference Official Report*, ed. by J. H. Oldham (Willett, Clark & Company, 1937), pp. 75–112.

3. Thomas Aquinas, *Summa Theologica* II–II. 66. 7.

4. See article by S. L. Parmar, *The Ecumenical Review*, Jan. 1974.

5. *The New York Times*, March 15, 1974.

6 *The New York Times Magazine*, March 21, 1965.

Chapter VII. WHAT SHOULD BE LEARNED FROM THE INDOCHINA WAR

1. Townsend Hoopes, *The Limits of Intervention* (David McKay Company, Inc., 1969), p. 51. McNaughton's unfortunate death in an airplane accident in this country prevents our hearing more from him about his views.

2. The Pentagon Papers, *New York Times* edition, p. 580.

3. *Ibid.*, p. 255. This is referred to at several other points in that edition of the Papers.

4. Quoted in Hannah Arendt, *On Revolution* (The Viking Press, Inc., 1965), p. 15.

5. Quoted by Reinhold Niebuhr in *The Irony of American History* (Charles Scribner's Sons, 1962), p. 71.

6. Josiah Strong, *Our Country* (New York, 1885), Ch. XIII.

7. Quoted in Martin E. Marty, *Righteous Empire: The Protestant Experience in America* (The Dial Press, Inc., 1970), pp. 222–223.

8. John K. Fairbank, in *China Notes*, Spring 1970.

9. Roy A. Medvedev's *Let History Judge* (tr. by Colleen Taylor, ed. by David Joravsky and Georges Haupt [Alfred A. Knopf, Inc., 1972]), written on the basis of research done in Russia but published outside, brings together the evidence for horrors of Stalinism. It is confirmed by the more publicized book by Aleksandr I. Solzhenitsyn, *The Gulag Archipelago, 1918–1956*, tr. by Thomas P. Whitney (Harper & Row, Publishers, Inc., 1974). The great publicity for the latter has often failed to do justice to the changes that have come since Stalin.

10. See Kingman Brewster, Jr., "Reflections on Our National Purpose," *Foreign Affairs*, April 1972.

11. This is an important chapter in American religious history and needs to be recorded as fully as possible. I am indebted to an early article by James H. Smylie, "American Religious Bodies, Just War, and Vietnam," in *A Journal of Church and State*, Autumn 1969.

12. The Pentagon Papers, *New York Times* edition, pp. 234 ff.

13. Alan Paton, *Christianity and Crisis*, Sept. 30, 1974.

14. See the chapter on "Civil Religion in America" in Robert N. Bellah, *Beyond Belief: Essays on Religion in a Post-traditional World* (Harper & Row, Publishers, Inc., 1970). See also Bellah's *The Broken Covenant* (The Seabury Press, Inc., 1975), which is a more critical discussion of civil religion and illuminates the relation between civil religion and Biblical religion.

Chapter VIII. FACING THE GLOBAL THREATS TO HUMANITY

1. Robert I. Heilbroner's article "The Human Prospect," first published in *The New York Review of Books,* is now available in the volume *An Inquiry Into the Human Prospect* (W. W. Norton & Co., Inc., 1974).

2. Barbara Tuchman, *The Proud Tower* (Bantam Books, Inc., 1972).

3. Bertrand Russell, *Power: A New Social Analysis* (W. W. Norton & Company, Inc., 1938), p. 271.

4. Henri Bergson, *The Two Sources of Morality and Religion,* tr. by R. Ashley Audra *et al.* (Henry Holt & Company, Inc., 1935), p. 69.

5. Before his death in 1941, Bergson was on the point of becoming a Christian, but it was not made public because of his loyalty to the Jewish people who were at that time victims of the Nazis.